The Secret CREATIONS of GOD

By Alan Casto

xulon PRESS

TABLE OF CONTENTS

INTRODUCTION

To understand the mystery of God's creations, I was taken on a trip in a time capsule, which was the word of God, into the secret creations of God. I used the illustration of a time capsule because that is what it felt like to me. I was traveling into the realm of the Spirit through time with the Holy Spirit, where I was showed the five creations of God. In the beginning of the creation of the original earth, there was a mystery showing what really happened. Verse 1 stands alone because there is a separation of time that consist of many years between the first two verses in Genesis 1:1, 2.

The Holy Spirit caused me to look at these two verses in a different way than what I was used to. First, the Holy Spirit reminded me that God never creates things imperfect, as (vs. 2) seems to infer. God is a creator of perfect things. He knows what they are to look like before He creates them. Therefore

God creates all things with perfection in all His creations. This fact about God is the determining factor that caused me to look for answers why those two verses were so different.

(Vs. 1) is making a statement that the heavens and the earth are complete structures of God's greatness, but the second verse is describing the earth as not being complete. (Vs. 2) says that the earth was void, without form, and it was covered over by water. The Holy Spirit showed to me that there was something missing in Moses' description of those two verses. If (vs. 1) is describing (vs. 1) creation, then God created it as a big mess? I was a little bit confused by these two verses, therefore I was not satisfied that those two verses belonged together. The more I looked at them, the more I was confused about them.

I gave up, because in my own mind, I could not figure them out. "Holy Spirit, please show me what I am missing!"

"Here is wisdom," the Holy Spirit said unto me. "There is a gap in time between those two verses that Moses did not reveal unto his readers because he was not told to reveal it to them, when he was writing his book."

The Bible is not written like other books because God instructs His prophets to write them in a special format, so that many secret messages can only be understood by His true followers. To the rest of the world it seems to be foolishness, because they do not care for the things of God. The first verse that you see refers to the heavens and the earth that were created in the beginning of their time, many years before (vs. 2) came into existence. The original heavens and earth were created perfect, because that is who God is: a creator of perfect things. So the key to unlock this mystery is in the knowledge of God Himself. To unlock its mystery requires a personnel relationship with God's Son, which gives that person access to God the Father, who gives us wisdom to understand His mysteries regarding His holy Word.

Through the Holy Spirit, I was given knowledge concerning the mystery of the first two verses. The first verse, **Genesis 1:1 "In the beginning God created the heavens and the earth,"** is telling us that God created the heavens and the earth many years ago. In the beginning, God created them perfect. But in (vs. 2), something happened to the earth to cause it to be in a big mess: *Genesis 1:2 "The earth was without form, and void; and darkness was on the face of the deep."*

In this book, I will give you the opportunity to travel in time with me, to see the five creations of God. It was an experience that changed my way of thinking, also the way I studied the word of God. I asked the Lord to help me to understand the first three chapters of Genesis, because I knew that I was missing something when I was studying them. He taught me how to look past my natural way of thinking by allowing my spirit to receive instruction from the Holy Spirit directly through His still, small voice. The more I studied the first two chapters, the more revelation I received from the Holy Spirit. I was then taken on a trip through the different dimensions of God's creations. This trip changed my way of thinking when I saw the **secrets** of the creations of God. It changed me into a man who wants to know God in a deeper way, so that I might know Him by His creative powers, who created all things according to His purpose. He showed me three different levels of creations in the first three chapters of Genesis, which encompassed a span of million of years.

There are key **secrets** in His Word that can give you wisdom, in understanding how these creations came into being. The information that I received about these subjects took me by surprise as I studied them in the spirit. As I began to study with the Holy Spirit teaching me, I was shown many **secrets** in the word of God that gave me the answers for those questions. It was so mind-boggling that I could only study it for a short amount of time, because of my former teaching on this subject. Who was I to question the almighty God!? I had to accept His answers in faith. Everything began to make sense to me then. What a mighty God we serve! There are many **secrets** in God's creations throughout the Bible that will blow your mind if you look at them with an open mind. The **secrets** that I will reveal to you in this book will bring new insights into the creations of God that maybe you have not heard about before in your lifetime.

If you are willing to take a trip with me through the Bible, you will be able to see how God really made His creations. This trip will take us back in time to the very beginning of time, where God created the earth in its original state. Then we will travel to the different creations from that time to the future, even beyond the time in which we now live. There are five different times that the earth will be made new again! This might surprise you until you read the whole book, then you will have a better understanding of what I meant by that statement. By taking this trip with me, you will see what happened between the first two verses of Genesis Chapter 1. There is a very large number of years between those two verses, possibly million of years. If that is not hard enough to understand, I will show you two other creations in the first two Chapters of Genesis! On this journey, you will be able to see the creations of God in a new light, apart from popular belief.

It is vitally important that you read my whole book before you pass any judgment against what I just stated. Believe me, I had a hard time seeing the whole picture of God's creations also! It took me a lot of prayer and studying the Bible before my eyes were opened to these **secrets** that were revealed unto me. In this book, I will talk to you about the fall of Lucifer and what his kingdom might have looked like before Genesis 1:1. He was already a fallen angel before his appearance in the Garden of Eden. I am sure that this journey into time will keep you in suspense as we travel back and forth in God's vast domain. There are many things to see, so I am sure that it will surprise you. Buckle up, because it is a long ride. After I finished this book, I received a revelation about the second coming of Christ, so I added it in the second part of this book.

Chapter One

THE FIRST CREATION OF GOD REVEALED AND THE FIRST FLOOD

To all you who are curious to know how the creations of God came into being, this is the book you should read. I found myself in this situation when I asked the Lord a question about the creation of our earth. I used to think that the First Chapter of Genesis was repeated in the Second Chapter, until the Holy Spirit began to teach me how to study in a new dimension of understanding in the word of God. I was taken on a journey through the Bible that changed my view on how to study and brought me to a new level of under-standing in a new dimension that I never experienced.

The Lord our God is a God of creations. He is the only one who can create things out of nothing. My little mind in its natural state of mind could not even begin to understand His creative power. Yes, it takes more than that, so I needed the power of His Holy Spirit to teach me how to study in my innermost being. Everyone who is born again has that ability to be able to do this. One day as I was asking Him a question about the creations of God, He instructed me to write this book. The Holy Spirit is now my best friend because He lives inside me. After all, the Holy Spirit was there in the beginning of all the creations of God, so I asked the Holy Spirit many questions as I was studying the word of God.

As I was writing this book, I was not alone, because the Holy Spirit was teaching me what to write. He taught me how to understand the creations of God because He was a part of them from the beginning of time. There is no way that I could have understood these things on my own, especially without the Holy Spirit's help. In this book, I will be talking to Him just as if I was talking to you, while you are reading this book, because the Holy Spirit is a real person who is a part of the Godhead.

I cannot take any credit for the things that I am writing because I have received these things from the Holy Spirit. Many **secrets** were revealed unto me on this journey. The more I studied about the creations, the more I found out how little I understood them. It took a long time for me to finally understand what the Holy Spirit was trying to teach me about God's creations. It really surprised me.

My first question to God was in the first verse, **Genesis 1:1 "In the beginning God created the heavens and the earth."** When was the beginning of time, Lord? Was this the first creation, before the chaos in the second verse of that chapter? The Holy Spirit took me on a journey to a new level of understanding in another dimension in the spiritual realm. He showed me some **secrets** that opened my mind to understand how many creations God had. The journey that the Holy Spirit and I went on in this book was a journey that very few people can know unless they have read this book. It is a journey that goes all the way back in the past, to the very beginning of time.

From there, the Holy Spirit took me to the other four creations of God, all the way to the future and then to the end of time as we know it. I will be talking back and forth with the Holy Spirit on this journey because He is the one in charge of it, not me. I know very little about the universe of the Creator my God, but God's Holy Spirit does. So I ask anyone who reads this book to buckle up as you take this journey into the spiritual realm.

Genesis 1:1 "In the beginning God created the heavens and the earth." This for sure is the first creation of God. It happened before the chaos in the next verse. Million of years ago, God created the heavens and the earth. They were created without the sun, moon or stars at that time. The Holy Spirit showed me that they (the sun, moon, stars) were not created until the second creation of God, which happened in the following verses of that same chapter.

This is what some people call the gap theory. But there is much more to the story than that. You will find more about this theory as you read this whole book. There is a gap in time, as I pointed out in this first chapter already. Moses, in Genesis, made a powerful statement in the first verse, where he described what God did in the beginning of time; **Genesis 1:1 "In the beginning <u>God created the heavens and the earth."</u>** But in the second verse he goes on to tell the story of what happened to the earth after the first flood that came on the earth. *Genesis 1:2 "The earth was without form, and void; and darkness was on the face of the deep."*

Then he tells us how God restored it back to its original state. By looking at the first two verses, I discovered there must be some more clues to why the earth was messed up in (vs. 2). God does not create things that are in chaos, but He can turn things that are in chaos into things of beauty. There is new meaning as the Holy Spirit enlightens scripture's true meaning. In *Genesis 1:2 "The earth was without form, and void; and darkness was on the face of the deep,"* the Holy Spirit revealed to me that there was a gap in time, between those two verses. I just wanted to know for sure if there was a gap between the first two verses. I knew in my heart that the Bible was true. I know that there are no mistakes in God's word, because God's word is always true. After all, He created everything that was ever made. I was confused when I read the second verse also: *Genesis 1:2 "The earth was without form, and void; and darkness was on the face of the deep."*

The **next clue** is in this second verse: If God created the heavens and the earth, why did (vs. 2) say that it was a total mess? My next request for the Holy Spirit was to show me what happened to the earth that caused it to become such a mess in (vs. 2). For me to understand this complex question, I had no choice but to rely on the guidance of the Holy Spirit. Why did God create the heavens and the earth in (vs. 1), then in (vs. 2) the earth "**was without form, and void;** *and darkness was on the face of the deep"*? This did not make any sense to me.

Then He instructed me to look a little bit closer at what that verse says: "What do you see after the 'void'?" Why, I see **darkness** on the face of the deep! I see the earth did not have any form because it was covered over with water. The water looked like it was frozen over so that it looked like a mirror, as if I could see a face! The secret to knowing about God's creation is all in His word, but to understand them, the Holy Spirit was to be my teacher, not man or other theology of man. Everything that God creates is good -- just look in Genesis: "**Genesis 1:1 "In the beginning God created the heavens and the earth."** He did not create it in vain, He created it to be inhabited. *Isaiah 45:18 "For thus says the Lord,* **Who created the heavens**, *Who is God,* **Who formed the earth** *and made it,* **Who established it**, **Who did not create it in vain**, **Who formed it to be inhabited**; *I am the Lord, there is no other."*

I asked the Holy Spirit to show me what that first creation looked like, who lived on it, and why it was destroyed, causing it to be in such a big mess in (vs. 2). The Holy Spirit began to teach me things that literally blew my mind. I was dumbfounded at how little I knew about the creations of God. I was taught that I needed to put away my childish way of thinking. I needed to trust His teaching because He gets all of

His instruction from God. There is no way of under-standing how God created this universe except by listening to His Spirit. Everybody seems to limit God in His ability to create only our universe. Well, I have got good news for you: God has been in existence for-ever. That alone is way beyond what our human minds can comprehend. God does not just float around in space doing nothing. If we were to look deeper into the word of God, we would find out some things about God that would amaze us. Take this, for instance: God was so bored one time, He needed to take a rest, so He decided to make a footstool for Himself. *Isaiah 66:1 "Thus says the Lord: 'Heaven is My throne, And* **the earth is My footstool.'"** (I did not say that; He did.) (Isaiah 45:18) "*Who did not create it in vain, Who formed it to be inhabited; I am the Lord, there is no other."*

The Holy Spirit took me on a trip through the word of God so that I could see the five creations that God had made. I did not see the first creation in the natural, but through His word I could see it in the spiritual realm. Another **secret clue**: *Psalm 104:1-9 "Bless the Lord, O my soul! O Lord my God, You are very great: You are clothed with honor and majesty, (vs. 2) Who cover Yourself with light as with a garment,* **Who stretch out the heavens like a curtain**. *(vs. 3) He lays the beams* *of His upper chambers in the waters, Who makes the clouds His chariot, Who walks on the wind, (vs. 4) Who makes His angel spirits, His ministers a flame of fire. (vs. 5)* **You who laid the foundations of the earth, So that it should not be moved forever,** *(vs. 6)* **You covered it with the deep as with a garment; The waters stood above the mountains.** *(vs. 7) At Your rebuke they fled; At the voice of Your thunder they hastened away. (vs. 8) They went up over the mountains; They went down into the valleys, To the place which You founded for them. (vs. 9) You have set a boundary that they may not pass over, That they may not return to cover the earth."*

David saw something in the spirit in these verses. In (vs. 2), he saw God "*stretch out the heavens like a curtain*" then in (vs. 5), he saw God "*laid the foundations of the earth.*" "Holy Spirit," I asked, "what does all of this mean?"

The Holy Spirit said, "David was allowed to see certain things in his spirit, something like I am showing you. He was shown the very first creation and how it was laid; then he was shown how it was covered over with water, but he was not given the reason why that happened."

David witnessed these acts in his spirit so that he could write them down. In these first few verses, David was able to see in his spirit the very first creation of God. It did not stop there, because in the next few verses that followed he was able to see in the spirit a flooding of the earth, where the earth was covered with water. Think about that for a moment. David was not given insight into what took place on the earth during that first creation. But he was not given insight into why those three creations ended in floods. **First**, he talked about God's goodness and majesty, then in (vs. 2) he saw "*Who stretch out the heavens like a curtain.*" He then saw God lay the foundations of the earth. Why would God lay the foundations of the earth and then cover the earth with water to destroy His beautiful creation?

David saw the gap between the first two verses of Genesis, right here in the verses of Psalm 104:5, 6. (vs. 5), "*You who* **laid the foundations** *of the earth, So that it should not be moved forever,*" David saw the first creation of God, then he saw the first flood of the earth in (vs. 6): "**You covered it with the deep as with a garment**; *The waters stood above the mountains.*" These two verses compare with the first two verses of Genesis to a T.

David saw the earth created first, then he saw it covered over with water, the same way as Moses did, but was not given the reason why the earth was covered over with water. I then asked the Holy Spirit to give me another **secret** clue, so that I could see why the earth ended that way. Then I needed to know what the earth really looked like before it was flooded. There is a mystery within these nine verses that shows us the first three creations of God. The Bible is written in such a way that if you read it with just your natural mind, you would miss what is being said. I have read this passage probably more than twenty times over the last sixty years, but it was not until the year 2010 that the Holy Spirit was able to help me see something that was hidden in these passages in Psalm 104:1-9. In these nine verses, God reveals to David the first three creations, written in a secret code so that no one could see them unless they were given their meaning by the Holy Spirit, who is the only one who knows their meaning. David was able to see in the spirit **the first three creations in these nine verses**. In the first five verses, he saw the First Creation of God. Then in (vs. 6), he saw the earth that God created, being flooded with water even over the mountains.

Then in **(vs. 7),** he saw the Second Creation in Genesis 1:2, 3, where God made the dry land appear. But then in **(vs. 8),** he saw the waters flood the earth for the second time. Then he saw the earth flooded for the last time in the third creation in (vs. 9), when he saw the promise of God to Noah that God would not flood the whole earth again.

When I read those verses, this time the Holy Spirit began to open my eyes of understanding so that I could see the first three creation in these nine verses. "O Lord, the first creation was made beautiful then you covered it over with water. Could I ask you why You covered it over with water?" The Holy Spirit showed me why this happened in Isaiah. The Holy Spirit reminded me that Lucifer was already a fallen angel in Genesis 1:2, so He said to me that Lucifer before his fall was a bright light himself. His name, Lucifer, means Day Star. His kingdom in the beginning of time was on this earth, as well as in the air. The reason the earth had no sun was because Lucifer's brightness was on the earth at that time. But when he rebelled against God, he became darkness. Then the earth had no light because Lucifer lost his brightness. Then God flooded the earth with water. It was at that time that the earth had an ice age, because there was no light on it. It stayed that way until God brought light on it by His Son, in Genesis 1:3. Here is **another secret** to the puzzle: What happened to the earth in the next verse?

Genesis 1:2 "The earth was without form, and void; and darkness was on the face of the deep." There is no way that the second verse is the description of what the earth looked like in its original creation. God did not create the earth in that condition!

The secret is revealed later in the Bible, as what happened between those two verses. Everything that God creates is always good. He does not create things that are messed up, like the second described it. By the way, where did the darkness come from? Now it is time for me to show you another piece of the puzzle.

Isaiah 14:12, 13 (vs. 12) *"How you are fallen from heaven, O* **Lucifer***, son of the morning! How* **you are cut down to the ground***, You who weakened the nations! (vs. 13) For* **you have said in your heart: I will ascend into heaven***, I will* **exalt my throne above the stars of God; I will also sit on the mount of the congregation** *On the farthest sides of the north."* Right here is a secret clue to why the earth ended in chaos and darkness, in Genesis 1:2. Many people take these verses in Isaiah out of context. These verses are being used to compare the king of Babylon to what happened to Lucifer in the very first creation, before the second verse in Genesis 1. Isaiah was talking to the kingdom of Babylon and its people in chapter 14. *Isaiah 14:3,4 "(vs. 3) It shall come to pass in the day Lord gives you rest from your sorrow, and from your fear and the hard bondage in which you were made to serve, (vs. 4) that* **you will take up this**

proverb against the king of Babylon, and say: '*How the oppressor has ceased, the golden city ceased!*'"

Then when I read Isaiah 14:12, 13, Isaiah was telling the kingdom of Babylon that the same thing that happened to Lucifer is going to happen to their kingdom. Within these few verses are an important secret clue about Lucifer. Lucifer was already a fallen angel when he appeared in Genesis 3:1, so I believe that Isaiah was revealing a hidden secret in these verses, by revealing what happened to Lucifer in the very beginning of time. Isaiah was talking to the kingdom of Babylon very strongly in the first eleven verses, then he talks to them about what had already happened to Lucifer before his fall and after his fall. Then Isaiah went back to show the kingdom of Babylon that they would be like Lucifer in the end.

The **key secret** is in "*(vs. 13) For* **you have said in your heart: I will ascend into heaven**, *I will* **exalt my throne above the stars of God.**" Lucifer fell because of pride in his heart. Isaiah was explaining to the Babylonians that just as Lucifer was being prideful in his heart, they too were doing the same thing. Babylon was also going to fall like Lucifer fell.

Isaiah **14:12, 13,** is telling us and the Babylonians who Lucifer was: "*son of the morning!*" during his reign over the first creation of God. He told them how he has fallen from heaven, then how he was **"cut down to the ground."** Then he said what Lucifer did to the nations. What nations was Isaiah talking about?

The **key secret** to theses verses is to keep them in the right context. Like I said, Isaiah started talking to the Babylonians, then in the verses above he talks about Lucifer. He was telling them that they too would be cut down and fall just like Lucifer did. To help you understand these scriptures, I will try to paraphrase them for you in my own words. My how you have fallen from heaven "O **Lucifer**, *son of the morning!*" You were cut down to the ground because you weakened the nations that you were ruling over, you were bright like the morning, until you fell.

1. Sin was in your heart because you said: (vs. 13) "*For* **you have said in your heart: I will ascend into heaven**, *I will* **exalt my throne above the stars of God; I will also sit on the mount of the congregation** *On the farthest sides of the north.*" In all of your power, Lucifer, you were cast down to the earth along with your kingdom, your light became darkness at the end of your reign.

Lucifer had a kingdom on the earth during the first creation of God. When he rebelled against God, his kingdom fell according to Isaiah, right after he said these important words: "*For* **you have said in your**

heart: I will ascend into heaven, *I will* **exalt my throne above the stars of God."** *Genesis 1:2 "The earth was without form, and void;* **darkness** *was on the face of the deep."* The Holy Spirit showed me that this **darkness** was none other than Satan himself, who is darkness because of his rebellion against God. Now that I have showed to you that the first creation was made well before the fall of Lucifer, I would like for you to see what Lucifer's kingdom might have looked like before his fall.

This now brings us to the point: What kind of cities were there? Were there any animals, or creatures, or possibly humans of some sort? Maybe on the first creation there could have been dinosaurs, large reptiles, I am not sure of these things, but I do have some other things the prophets saw. *"You who weakened the nations!"* Lucifer had some kind of nations under his rule. He had other angels he was over, because when he fell about one-third of the angels fell with him. Many people have applied those scriptures in Isaiah 14 to the future in Revelation, but I have a problem with that theory, because Lucifer was already a fallen angel at the end of the first creation of God, as I established earlier. What did Lucifer's kingdom look likes before his fall? The Holy Spirit allowed me to take a trip in my time capsule (which was the word of God) to see in the spirit what He was showing me about this first creation. The sun, moon, and stars were not seen here on this journey when I arrived on the earth in the first creation in the spirit. I saw that they did not exist there because they were not created until after Genesis 1:14. There was light on the earth at this time when I landed there in the spirit. It was bright, but I saw no sun! The earth was beautiful everywhere I looked, but where was this light coming from?

I stepped out to see the amazing view of the earth. The air that I breathed was beyond description. It was the freshest air that I had ever breathed. The light that I saw was hard for me to understand -- how could it shine without the sun? It was the strangest thing I ever saw. It had to be coming from a source that was stronger than the sun. It was greater than the sun itself back in my days before this journey started.

The Holy Spirit said to me, "This is a time where Lucifer, which means 'Day Star,' was living on the earth. Before his fall he was the brightest light than any other angel. There was no need of the sun, moon or stars because of his brightness. He had a kingdom because he was the ruler of the earth in that duration of time."

There were no weeds in the gardens because there was no curse on the original earth. Then I saw all of the animals running wild, and they all got along real well. There were mountains, rivers, lakes, trees, grass, plus there was no pollution of any kind. I know that Lucifer was the ruler of this domain because the Bible tells us that he rebelled against God some time in this error of time. At this time, you might think that I am out of my mind, but be assured I am not. I will show you in the coming Chapters that there were things here in the First Creation that God pulled out of the earth in the Second Creation. I was not told too much about who or what was in his kingdom, but he had a throne and a kingdom many years ago. Many people think that Jeremiah was talking about the future in those scriptures, but I think that he saw back to the very beginning of time, because that would explain why the earth ended in chaos in Genesis 1:2. It made more sense to me as I was studying the scriptures.

Can you see it with me? I firmly believe that God would not create the earth to be in chaos, just to re-create it again. Why not make it perfect the first time? He did make it perfect in the very beginning of time. I know there are not many scriptures on this sub-ject, but as you can see, it does make sense if we study the scriptures in the spirit, with the Holy Spirit of God's guidance. We need to learn how to bypass the natural mind through the Spirit of God that is in us. I know that it is hard to understand these theories of the creation. That is why you must meditate in the spirit, relying on the Spirit of God for the revelation in His word. I was able to see a beautiful angel who stood out more than the other angels around me. There were cities with a kingdom from which this angel ruled.

I asked the Holy Spirit, "Who is this angel who is so beautiful, who rules over so many other angels?" My heart began to pound out of my chest when the Holy Spirit said to me, "This angel is Lucifer, who rules over this kingdom and over the other angels. It is good now, but I will show you what is to come!" I was filled with a heart full of fear for a moment. I could hardly speak as the sweat began to pour down my face. As I stood there, a cool breeze began to blow across my face. The Holy Spirit took me to a place in the spirit realm, to a place in Isaiah 14:12, 13. He told me that everything was about to change from this time forward. Pride filled Lucifer's heart until he rebelled against God. The Holy Spirit pointed this out to me.

Lucifer's kingdom was about to change. Look at *Isaiah 14:14, 15 -- "(vs. 14) I will ascend above the heights of the clouds, I will be like the Most High. (vs. 15) Yet you shall be brought down to Sheol, To the lowest depths of the pit."* All of those beautiful things I saw in the first creation were about to change because of Lucifer's rebellion against God. (vs. 12) *"O Lucifer, son of the morning! How you are cut down to the ground."* Darkness began to fall on the earth all around me as God's judgment fell on Lucifer, who was about to be reduced to a serpent. Watch what happened to his kingdom! The prophet Jeremiah, received things from God pertaining to Lucifer's kingdom. The angel of the Lord instructed me to enter my time capsule (which is the word) at this time, because the earth was about to be flooded for the first time. Through Jeremiah's writings in the next few verses, I was able to see all of these things with the Spirit's help. Every man along with every beast was gone. The birds fled before my eyes also. Darkness filled the earth in a moment of time, therefore there was no light anymore. The earth became void as the flood waters covered the earth, even over the mountains.

You will never begin to understand these things that I talked about so far unless you can see them in the spirit. I was unable to understand them until the Holy Spirit showed them unto me while I was in the Spirit. *Jeremiah 4:23-26 "I beheld the earth, and indeed it was without form, and void; And the heavens, they had no light. (vs. 24) I beheld the mountains, and indeed they trembled, And the hills moved back and forth. (vs. 25) I beheld, and indeed* **there was no man,** *And all the* *birds of the heavens had fled. (vs. 26) I beheld, and indeed the fruitful land was a wilderness, And* **all its cities were broken down** *At the presence of the Lord, By His fierce anger."*

{This scripture 4:23-26 is referring to the beginning of time. These verses are not talking about Noah's flood for sure; because if you look at them closely, they do not compare at all.} Again, I was given information about what took place in the First Creation of God in Genesis 1:1. Jeremiah gave me some key data about the first creation of God in these few verses. The Holy Spirit pointed out to me the reason why the first creation ended in chaos in Genesis 1:2. He was cast down to the ground, where he was reduced to the form of a serpent. He became known as darkness instead of light. His darkness was noticed in Genesis 1:2. The earth was flooded over completely. Right before my eyes everything was destroyed and the earth became void, full of darkness. His kingdom lasted till the flood in Genesis 1:2, although he was not destroyed, nor his followers, because they were spirit beings. His earthly kingdom was destroyed completely. This tells me that the first creation was inhabited with men of some kind, plus there were at least birds there. Then God was angry enough to destroy Lucifer's kingdom. Lucifer's rebellion was the reason

God flooded the earth for the first time, causing it to be void and full of darkness. What a sight it must have been. It would have been good if we were able to see them like Jeremiah saw them. Jeremiah saw Genesis 1:1, then he saw why the earth became that way in the following verses. All of Lucifer's cities were broken down. It looked like a wilderness from that time on.

This took place because of the rebellion of Lucifer and his followers. His kingdom was wiped out *"At the presence of the Lord, By His fierce anger."* (vs. 26). God was not pleased with Lucifer any longer. He also pointed out that no man was left, and the birds fled also. He showed me that once the land was fruitful, but now it had become a wilderness, also every city was broken down. This was done by the Lord in His anger. It happened because Lucifer rebelled against God, as we have already studied. This First Creation of God was for sure an interesting experience to go through. It lasted for many years until the rebellion of Lucifer's kingdom came to an end. I do not have much scripture on what happened to the earth in its original creation, but with the Holy Spirit's teaching I was able to see it in the spirit.

This brings us to *Genesis 1:2, "The earth was without form, and void; and darkness was on the face of the deep."* When God flooded the earth in the first creation, we are not told how long the earth was in that condition in this verse. There were many years between the first two verses of Genesis 1. During the transition of the earth being flooded over with water until Genesis 1:3, the earth could have been in an ice age period. The earth was without any light, thus, it would have been very cold without any heat from the light source that was in the first creation. This theory then would explain how the earth was in an ice age, according to modern science beliefs.

This first creation of God was an eye opener for me. I spent a long time studying the first three chapters of Genesis, plus the other books of the Bible. This was for sure a wild ride for me, as I am sure it was for you too, because there were things that I was not familiar with. Hold on to your hats. The next chapter is going to be the same way.

Chapter Two

THE SECOND CREATION OF GOD

C ome with me now to the second creation of God. The earth was a total mess here in Genesis 1:2: "The earth was without form, and void; and darkness was on the face of the deep."

In this Second Creation, I was given more secrets that surprised me in my traditional teaching on this creation, I was taught that this was the only creation of our earth. I was taught that Adam and Eve were formed from the dust of the earth in this Second Creation.

As we have already seen, this theory is not true, because we have seen that the earth was created in the beginning of time before the second verse came into being. In Genesis 1:2, God was going to make or recreate the earth anew. He was about to add a few more elements to it that were not a part of the original earth in the beginning of time.

In my traditional teaching on this creation, I was taught that the earthly man and woman were a part of this creation, but there are *secrets* that may change your mind on this matter. It required me to take a deep study into the first three chapters of Genesis, which helped me to have a better understanding of the <u>first three creations of God</u>. Through my own personal study on these subjects, I was allowed to see *secrets* that opened my spiritual mind into a new level of understanding about the mystery of God's creations. God created the earth to last forever, according to His word, so God the Father, God the Son, and the Holy Spirit showed up in (vs. 2) to bring the earth back to a livable place again. *Genesis 1:2: "The earth was without form, and void; and darkness was on the face of the deep. And the Spirit of God was hovering over the face of the waters."*

Now that I have showed to you what happened to the original earth -- which was created perfect but now was destroyed because of Lucifer's rebellion against God -- I would like to show you the Second Creation of God. This creation of God is a creation that is misunderstood by most people because of their lack of knowledge. They may not have been shown the secrets that are hidden within the scriptures. The first thing God did was to send His Spirit to the earth to prepare it to be changed into something good, as you will be able to see starting in (vs. 3).

Then God called for the light to come. This is where Jesus Christ came to be the light of the world, because God always uses His Son in all of His creations. (Remember, Lucifer was the light on the earth in the first creation until his rebellion against God.)

First, let me tell you something important that you must do so that you will be able to understand where I am coming from as I teach you these things. <u>You must pray in the Spirit to God for wisdom,</u> so that you will be able to see what the Spirit is trying to teach you concerning the creations of God. Pray for understanding within your spiritual man, do not rely on your natural mind, but rely on the Holy Spirit as your guide.

This Second Creation of God goes from Genesis 1:2 to Genesis 2:3. The number of years that it lasted is not known for sure, but it lasted a long time because it was in this creation that the sun, moon, and stars where created (Genesis 1:16, 17). The earth was without light or heat, plus it was covered over with water for a long period of time, possibly million of years (we are not told exactly how long). Genesis 1:2: "The earth was without form, and void; and darkness was on the face of the deep. And the Spirit of God was hovering over the face of the waters."

So in Genesis 1:2 the earth was a total mess. It had to be in an ice age condition before the Holy Spirit of God came on the scene, because there was no light or sun to keep the water from freezing. "…**darkness was on the face of the deep.**" Lucifer was no longer light but darkness. That is why the earth had the "darkness." His rebellion caused him to become darkness in this second creation. The "face of the deep" was like a mirror because of the frozen waters. If you were to look at it, you would see your own face. Another key verse: the waters had a face when the brightness of the Holy Spirit moved over the frozen waters. It was like looking into a mirror. The Spirit was moving over the frozen water to get it ready for God. He changed the ice back into water, so that it could be put back to its original places. **Job 38:29, 30 (29) From whose womb comes the ice? And the frost of heaven, who gives it birth? (30) The waters harden like stone, <u>And the surface of the deep is frozen</u>.**" God was asking Job a lot of questions. This verse could be referring to an ice age at the end of the first creation. God was not pleased that the earth was such a mess. I am sure of that, so God was about to bring back the beauty that the earth had before the fall of

Lucifer. During the ice age between the first two creations, God preserved all of the vegetation that had seeds in the ground's surface during that time, so that He could bring them forth again in the second creation. All of the beasts and living things that had bones were preserved also in the ground, as we will find out shortly in the next few verses. I am not really told how long the time span was between the first two verses; I believe that it was many years. *"And the Spirit of God was hovering over the face of the waters."* God's Spirit was moving over the waters, waiting to create things for God in (vs. 3).

Here I was, on the earth in my time capsule, looking through the windows, only to see total darkness. What happened to the earth? It used to be full of light and beauty. It was a good thing that my time capsule was waterproof, because all I could see was water all around me on every side.

"Look over there," the Holy Spirit said to me.

I looked on the waters, then I could see Him moving over the face of the waters I just heard a voice calling from the darkness, which sounded like a voice as loud as the thunders from a storm. It was God's voice speaking, at which time all of heaven and the earth stood at attention.

**Genesis 1:3 "Then God said, 'Let there be light';
and there was light."** God spoke the words: **"Let
there be light."** If the sun was not created, where did
this light come from? That is a good question. God
does not need the sun to get light. After all, God is
light. God is the creator of faith. When God speaks a
word of creation, it comes from within Himself. God
could see the light before it appeared, because He
already has the light within Himself. All God had to do
was to speak it forth: **"Let there be light"; and there
was light.** The light came forth. God's Son, who is the
light of the world, came forth. He was bright enough
to light the universe as well as the earth. David had
something to say: **Psalm 74:15, 16 "(vs. 15) You
broke open the fountain and the flood; You dried
up mighty rivers. (vs. 16) The day is Yours, the
night also is Yours; <u>You have prepared the light
and the sun.</u>"** David saw that the light came from
God. He also saw that it was God who made the sun.
David was given the secret insight that there was a
light other than the sun. The verse did not say that the
sun created the light, it said God prepared the light
and then made the sun.

In this Second Creation of God, God needed to
make the sun, moon, and stars because the spiritual male and female He was going to create were

not going to be bright glowing beings like the angels in the last creation. It was God's purpose to create a light source that would heat up the earth's atmosphere, so that the vegetation and animals could live and grow. So God made the sun, moon, and stars in Genesis 1:14.

In **Psalm 104:10-12** -- "(vs. 10) *He sends the springs into the valleys; They flow among the hills. (vs. 11) They give* **drink to every** **beast of the field;** **The** **wild donkeys** *quench their thirst. (vs. 12) By them the* **birds of the heavens** *have their home; They sing among the branches.*"

David was able to see all of God's creations. He saw things that were made in the first creation in(vs. 10-18), then in (vs. 19-29) he saw the Second Creation of God; then in (vs. 30) he sees the Third Creation of God being made. The key secret (vs. 13, 14, 19, 23, 29, and 30). "**(vs. 13) He waters the hills from His** **upper chambers; The earth is satisfied with the** **fruit of Your works.**" This verse pertains to the first two creations, because in the third creation, the earth was watered from the midst of the earth. It did not rain from the upper chambers until the flood of Noah. The secret key in (vs. 14) proves that there were men on the earth in those two creations. "**(vs. 14) He caused** **the grass to grow for the cattle, And vegetation** for the service <u>of man</u>, **That they may bring forth food from the earth."**

The next key secret is in "**(vs. 19) He appointed the moon for seasons; The sun knows its going down."** David talks about the second creation in this verse, because that is when the sun was created. Then in (vs. 23), we see proof that earthly men existed. **"(vs. 23) Man goes out to his work And to his labor until evening."** This could not be talking about the spirit man that God created in the Second Creation, so that means David is referring to an earthly being, because when you look at (vs. 29), they return to dust. The spirit man that God created was made a spirit like Him, not of dust.

Now there is another secret key verse: "**(vs. 29) You hide Your face, they are troubled; <u>You take away their breath, they die and return to their dust."</u>** This means that there were earthly men in the second creation, because in the next verse I will show you another secret key verse to help us to understand God's creations. "**<u>(vs. 30) You send forth Your Spirit, they are created; And You renew the face of the earth."</u>** Now this is a very important verse in unlocking a **secret mystery key** of understanding. David is telling us that this is the place that takes us into the third creation of God. This verse takes us to where the Third Creation starts in Genesis 2:4; "**<u>they</u> <u>are created</u>**" in (vs. 30) above referees to the earthly Adam and Eve. The earth is renewed in this chapter because the second creation ended in Psalm 104:29. The Third Creation of God starts in Genesis 2:4. This is what David saw in Psalm 104:30. God renews the earth for the third time. God, who created the earth in the beginning of time, was not going to let the earth remain in a chaos condition any longer in this Second Creation. No sir, God created the earth to be inhabited, so now He started the second creation to be renewed by speaking into the earth's atmosphere: **"Let there be light."**

From this moment the earth began to take shape. This second creation was being renewed, whereas the First Creation was created out of nothing. In this First Chapter of Genesis, the word *create* was only used three times; (vs. 1, 21, 27). (Vs. 1) was used for the First Creation of God. The word *create* in (vs. 21, 27) was used to create things that were not a part of the First Creation. Or maybe God just wanted to show His creative power in the Second Creation. I am not sure, but God is the creator of everything, regardless of how it is created or made. Everything else in this Second Creation of God was brought out of the earth. **Genesis 1:3 "Then God said, 'Let there be light';**

and there was light." All of a sudden, I could see clearly. As a matter of fact, it hurt my eyes because of its brightness. In the splendor of this bright light, I noticed that it was the same light that was in my last stop -- you know, the First Creation. The light in this Second Creation came from Jesus Christ, because the sun was not yet created until (vs. 16). The light came the moment that God spoke it out of His mouth. God saw that the light was good. As I looked from my capsule, I could see God taking the light and darkness to divide them into two parts.

Genesis 1:4, 5 "And God saw the light that it was good; and God divided the light from the darkness. God called the light Day, and the darkness He called Night. So the evening and the morning were the first day." In the First Creation in the beginning of time there was no night mentioned at all. In the Second Creation of God, the night and darkness are mentioned for the first time. Now that Lucifer had become a fallen angel, the darkness appeared on the earth for the first time.

Ephesians 6:12 "For we do not wrestle against flesh and blood, but against principalities, against powers, against the **rulers of darkness** *of this age, against spiritual hosts of wickedness in the heavenly places."*

The first day of this creation was now complete. Now I was waiting to see what the second day would bring forth. As I waited patiently for the second day, I saw God do some more dividing of the elements of the earth and the heavens, by reading His word. He divided the waters under heaven from the waters in the firmament above, in this second day of the creation.

Genesis 1:6 "Then God said, 'Let there be a firmament in the midst of the waters and let it divide the waters from the waters.'

As I watched in amazement, I saw God divide the two waters on the second day of the creation. I could hardly wait to see what the third day would bring. It was an amazing thing to see how the elements of the earth would obey the commands of God's voice, speaking unto them. Remember one thing: there is still no moon, sun, or stars in the first three days of this creation, yet there is day and night, without their help. The earth has to be very old in this second creation of God, because we know that the **sun, moon, and stars are eon years old. So please keep this in mind as we go through these scriptures.**

In this First Chapter of Genesis, Moses explains how God created the earth for the second time since the beginning of time. This is the time that God created the sun, moon, and the stars, as you will read in the next few verses. I know that the sun, moon, and stars have to be older than 6,000 years old, by all the reports that I have read over the years, in the present time I now live in. Now in this second creation in Genesis 1, there must be some kind of explanation as to why it is different from the creation that I read about in the second chapter of Genesis. I will talk about this later in another chapter in this book. As I was waiting in my time capsule, I was entering the third day of the second creation of God. As I looked out my window, something strange began to happen. I saw all of the waters flow into one place.

Listen to what God said: *Genesis 1:9, 10 "Then God said, 'Let the waters under the heavens be gathered together into one place, and let the dry land appear'; and it was so. And God called the dry land Earth, and the gathering together of the waters He called Seas, And God saw that it was good."* Finally the earth started to look like something I was used to. If I were able to, I would have stepped out of my time capsule to get a better look, but because I was on a pretend trip, I was not able to do so. In all the splendor of this creation, it was amazing to see the great power of the living God at work. With the earth separated from the waters, there was still something missing from the earth. I then heard God's voice speaking, like the noise of many waters, into the air.

*Genesis 1:11-13 "Then God said, '**Let the earth bring forth** grass, the herb that yields seed, and the fruit tree that yields fruit according to its kind, **whose seed is in itself**, on the earth'; (vs. 12) And **the earth brought forth** grass, the herb that yields seed according to its kind, and the tree that yields fruit, whose seed is in itself according to its kind. And God saw that it was good. (vs. 13) So the evening and the morning were the third day."*

The order of creation is sometimes misunderstood, therefore I must take a closer look at what God created within the duration of time they were created. **First**, it is established in the word of God, **Genesis 1:1 "In the beginning God created the heavens and the earth."** They (the heavens and the earth) were created to be inhabited, so I believe all creatures of the earth were created, plus the birds that did not have wings. Every living thing was created at that time. The strange thing that I noticed was that the sea creatures and the birds that had wings were not created until the Second Creation of God.

With the exception of the sea creatures and the winged birds, everything else in this Second Creation came into being by God pulling them out of the earth.

Look in: *Genesis 1:11-13.* What do you see or read there? God spoke, commanding the earth to bring forth grass, herbs, and fruit trees! A very important **secret** is in these few verses. What is this secret that I am talking about here? This **secret** is in the **seeds**! Everything listed here has its seed within itself, according to its kind. (Vs. 12) tells us that the earth brought forth all of those things that God required of it. Is this not amazing? God saw something in the earth that could not be seen with the naked eye, but God sees things in the spiritual realm with spiritual eyes. That is better than any x-ray machine could see!

You see, God already created these things in the First Creation, so when He destroyed the first creation with a flood, those creations were buried in the earth with their seeds in themselves. Now in this Second Creation, God commanded the earth to bring forth those items, grass, herbs, and fruit trees. Those creations were seeds lying dormant in the earth, waiting to come alive, breaking through the earth's surface when they heard the voice of their Maker calling them to come forth. (Remember: the earth was frozen over for many years for a reason; everything that was on the earth in that duration of time was frozen when God flooded it over with water, then there was darkness without any light whatsoever, thus there was no heat, causing the earth to go into an ice age, to pre-serve them for the Second Creation of God. The word of God did not say that it became frozen, but by the law of physics, the water on the earth had to become frozen because there was no heat source at that time.) This is why God did not have to create them in the Second Creation. Now in this Second Creation of God, God knew that the earth had these things already beneath its surface, because God sees things that we cannot see. To prove this, look at *Genesis 1:11*. Tell me, what do you see? I see God commanding the earth to bring forth things out of it. All of the things listed had seeds, each one according to its kind. They were buried beneath the earth's surface, so they could not have the life without the call of God. God spoke these words of life out of His mouth: *(vs. 11)* -- "**Let the earth bring forth grass**, *the herb that yields seed, and the fruit tree that yields fruit according to its kind,* **whose seed is in itself, on the earth'**; *and it was so."*

In the next verse, the earth brought those things forth. The **secret** is revealed in these scriptures that bring new meaning to the way we need to study. Two things need to be created in this Second Creation for these two reasons: if there were sea creatures in the very First Creation, their seeds would have been destroyed when the earth was frozen over before the Second Creation started. At that point they could not be re-created because their seeds died. But the ones in (vs. 11) had seeds that were protected by their hard shells from the elements outside of their surface, causing them to be preserved during the ice age at the end of the First Creation of God. The earth did what God commanded it to do: *(vs. 12) "And* **the earth brought** *forth grass, the herb that yields seed according to its kind, and the tree that yields fruit, whose seed is in itself according to its kind. (vs. 13) So the evening and the morning were the third day."* There was still something strange about the earth in this creation: there was light for the day, but there was still darkness for the night even though there was still no sun, moon, or stars as of yet in the heavens.

By the time I tried to figure things out, the fourth day began. I heard the voice of God speaking again. *Genesis 1:14,15 "Then God said, 'Let there be lights in the firmament of the heavens to divide the day from the night; and let them be for signs and seasons, and for days and years; (vs. 15) and let them be for lights in the firmament of the heavens to give light on the earth'; and it was so."*

In Genesis 1:3-5, God created a different light than what was described in the verses above. On the first day of God's creation, *Genesis 1:3 "Then God said,*

'Let there be light'; and there was light." The light that came here in verse 3 was none other than Jesus Christ. Note: *John 8:12 "Then **Jesus spoke** to them again, saying, 'I **am the light of the world**. He who follows Me shall not walk in **darkness**, but have the light of life.'"* When God said, "Let there be light," Jesus came as the light of the world. Jesus represented that light, therefore Satan represented the darkness.

As I said, the sun, moon, and stars were not created until Genesis 1:16, which we will look at next. There are different levels of the heavens, but I have not yet studied them all as of yet, so for now I will talk about the different lights that Moses talks about, here in this Second Creation of God. The first light is in Genesis 1:3. That light was Jesus Christ, as I already talked about in the last two paragraphs above. Let us read about the next lights that Moses talks about, in *Genesis 1:14, "Then God said, 'Let there be lights in the firmament of the heavens to divide the day from the night; and let them be for signs and seasons, and for days and years.'"* These lights are great lights made for the firmament of the heavens. Their purpose was to *"divide the day from the night; and let them be for signs and seasons, and for days and years."* Look at Psalm 136:5-9, *"(vs. 5) To Him who by wisdom made the heavens, For His mercy endures forever; (vs. 6)*

To **Him who laid out the earth above the waters**, *For His mercy endures forever; (Vs. 7) To Him who made* **great lights**, *For His mercy endures forever; (vs. 8) The sun to rule the day, For His mercy endures forever; ((vs. 9) The moon and* **stars** *to rule the night, For His mercy endures forever."* He talks about stars and great lights in these verses. What is the difference in them?

The stars were the lights that were set in the heavens to give light on the earth, as we can see in the next verse: *1:15, "and let them be for lights in the firmament of the heavens to give light on the earth."* I did notice that God was about to make two great lights in the next verse: *1:16, "Then God made two great lights: the greater light to rule the day, and the lesser light to rule the night. He made the stars also."*

As I looked out of my time capsule, I could see God placing them in the firmament of the heavens. (Gen.1:18, 19) *"And God saw that it was good. So the evening and morning were the fourth day."* Now the earth was looking better to me because I was used to seeing the sun, moon and stars before I left on this journey in my time capsule. It was in this Second Creation of God that all of these things were created or commanded to come forth out of the earth. Which means that the earthly man was not created at that time because the sun, moon, and stars are probably million of years old. For this reason, I believe that there are three different creations that Moses is talking about here in the first two Chapters of Genesis. That is the reason I am taking this trip back in time to see what happened. Scientist believe that the sun is eon of years old, so they could be right, because in my theory of these three creation that I have studied so far in Genesis chapter 1 and 2, they are divided by eon of years. I have already showed you the differences in the first part of this book. The Spirit of God is still moving over the earth during this Second Creation of God, awaiting God to speak the word so that He could move into action. The only things that was created out of nothing are found in these next few verses. May I bring to your attention something very important in the next few verses? God is going to create the second thing in this Second Creation of God. In (vs. 20), God is going to create an atmosphere for something to be created. He does this by speaking it out of His mouth, for with the tongue comes life or death. God first speaks out the things that He wants to happen. In the next verse the action of creation takes place.

Now let us talk about the **fifth day** of God's second creation. Again I heard God speak as I looked from my window of the time capsule. *Genesis 1:20, 21 "(vs. 20) Then God said, 'Let the waters abound with an* *abundance of living creatures, and let birds fly above the earth across the face of the firmament of the heavens.' (vs. 21) So* **God created** *great sea creatures and every living thing that moves, with which the waters abounded, according to their kind, and every winged bird according to its kind. And God saw that it was good."* God knew what He wanted to take place here. There is something to these verses, because God first set the atmosphere of what He saw in the Spirit by speaking what was to take place. He spoke to the waters to abound with an abundance of living creatures. God prepared the waters with an atmosphere, to receive sea creatures of every sort.

He prepared the earth as well as the heavens to allow themselves to be filled with the birds that fly. Now that the atmosphere was ready, God went into action: *Genesis 1:21 "So* **God created** *great sea creatures and every living thing that moves with which the waters abounded, according to their kind, and every winged bird according to its kind. And God saw that it was good."* All of these creatures were able to reproduce themselves because the waters abounded in producing the kinds of food to sustain life. God already spoke to the waters to do that very thing. Before these verses, everything came from the earth, but in these verses God created great sea creatures along with every living thing that moves in the water, and every winged bird. Maybe these creatures did not exist in the first creation, I was not told for sure, but God did have to create these creatures in verse 21.

The first thing that God created was in Genesis 1:1, which was the First Creation of God. The Bible mentions the word "created" in the first verse, which was used in creating the earth and the heavens. There are only two things that God created out of nothing in the Second Creation of God, which actually starts from Genesis 1:2 to 2:3.

The second time the word "created" is used is in (vs. 21), which is the first time the word "creation" was used in this Second Creation of God. In Genesis 1:21, God created the great sea creatures and every living thing that moves in the water, plus every winged bird. The third time the word "created" is used is in Genesis 1:27. "*So God created man.*" so why did I mention these things? I thought that it might bring some light on the word "create." Many things in this Second Creation of God were produced from things that were already in the earth that were preserved from the First Creation of God. Now in these next few verses, God commanded the earth to bring forth some other creatures. In all of these creations, I did notice one thing: "*(vs. 21) And God saw that it was good.*" Everything that God created looked good. That is why I say that there was a reason why the earth was in chaos in 1:2, where the second creation started.

Genesis 1:22, 23, "And God blessed them, saying, 'Be fruitful and multiply, and fill the waters in the seas, and let birds multiply on the earth.' So the evening and the morning were the fifth day."

God's blessings went out to all of these creatures that He created. How great is that? It is always great to be blessed by the Creator of the universe. To receive a blessing from God is a great honor as well as a great privilege to have, because God does not just give them to anybody. He only blesses those who He wants to bless. God echoed the words, *"Be fruitful and multiply, and fill the waters in the seas, and let birds multiply on the earth."* He told His created creatures to multiply to fill the earth, because He intended for the earth to be inhabited. That was God's purpose. All of these creatures that live in the water would not be destroyed in the second flood. I will discuss this later on in this book. Again, I find God speaking to the Holy Spirit what He wanted the earth to do. *Genesis 1:24, "Then God said, 'Let the earth bring forth the living creature according to its kind: Let the earth bring forth the living creature according to its kind: cattle and creeping thing and beast of the earth, each according to its kind;'*

and it was so." Again, God spoke to the earth, commanding it to bring forth all kinds of living things. God set the atmosphere, with faith calling things out of the earth that could not be seen with the natural eye. God saw those things in the Spirit, therefore He saw that it was good. Then God took action with the Son and Holy Spirit to make those things become reality. *Genesis 1:25, "And* **God made the beast of the earth** *according to its kind, cattle according to its kind, and everything that creeps on the earth according to its kind. And God saw that it was good."*

These beasts were hidden within the earth until God called the earth to bring them forth. I believe that these beasts existed in the First Creation, so when God destroyed it with the first flood, everything died and was buried deep in the earth. Their bones did not decay because they were in a deep freeze until the start of the Second Creation. I know that this theory of mine sounds crazy, but believe me, it sounded crazy to me to until I asked the Holy Spirit to reveal the meaning of these scriptures. God knew that those creatures were buried in the earth. That is why *"(vs. 24) Then God said,* **'Let the earth bring forth the living creature** *according to its kind: cattle and creeping thing and beast of the earth, each according to its kind'; and it was so."*

57

In this verse, God did not create them, but in the next verse, He did make them that came up out of the earth. The verse did not say in what form it brought the living creatures in, but in (vs. 25), God made each one of them, so He could have used the bones of each of them to do that very thing. I am not sure, but in Ezekiel, if you remember, there were dry bones that God used to make an army of men. Five days had passed already, which could be twenty-four-hour days as we know days, or a thousand days as one day is described by Peter in *2 Peter 3:8: "But, beloved, do not forget this one thing, that with the Lord one day is as a thousand years, and a thousand years as one day."*

I am not sure, but sense each day was mentioned as a day and night, so it probably was a literal day. That is all that counts. But at any rate, I was now expecting what was in store for the sixth day of God's second creation. After a good night's sleep, I was awakened by the sound of God's voice speaking to the earth. It was a bright morning at that as the rays of light came bursting into the window in my time capsule. When God speaks, all of creation listens. *Genesis 1:24, 25, (vs. 24) "Then God said, '***Let the earth bring forth the living creatures** *according to its kind: cattle, and creeping thing and beast of the earth, each according* *to its kind', and it was so. (vs. 25) And* **God made the beast of the earth according to its kind,** *cattle according to its kind, and everything that creeps on the earth according to its kind. And God saw that it was good."*

It was amazing to watch as God went to work, making all of these animals and creeping things. He first commanded the earth to bring them forth. I watched the substance of the earth begin to take on other forms of appearances, as God made all of the creatures from the earth. (In this second creation, it is possible that God created dinosaurs. This is just my guess, I have no proof except they did exist in some point in time.) Did you ever have some modeling clay when you were a child? What kind of things could you make from it? With any kind of imagination, you could make just about anything from it, although it might not be pretty. God took some of the earth into His hands and made all of the animals and creeping creatures come to life, according to His instructions. When God finished, He saw that it was good. Let us examine this creation very closely to see how it compares to the next creation in Genesis Chapter 2. You will be surprised when I reveal some more **secrets** of God's creation as you and I move forward on our journey through time.

Moses gives us an account of this second creation of God from Genesis 1:2 through 2:3, then he gives us an account of a third creation from Genesis 2:4 through the rest of the Bible, until the fourth creation, which we will talk about in another chapter. One of the **secrets** of the creations in the first chapter of Genesis, I found as I studied these verses closely. The **days in which God created different things in this second creation did not match the order of creation in the third creation in Genesis 2:4.** The **male and female were created in the sixth day of God's creation in the first chapter of Genesis.** The **man and the woman God formed from the dust of the earth in Genesis chapter 2 were created before everything else was created**. But in the **first Chapter,** they **were created after everything else**.

I was confused when I read those things, so I asked the Lord, "How can you explain these things to me?" The Holy Spirit began taking me through some scriptures in the Bible to show me some **secrets** that would open up my understanding on these matters. To understand the theory of these **two creations**, I was led to read them more closely. I was taken on a journey into the spiritual realm of understanding that changed my old way of thinking. He taught me that there was no way of understanding the creations of

God in my natural way of thinking. He taught me that there are key words to reveal **secrets** that unlock the realm of the spiritual understanding. We have already seen the very first creation of God in the first part of this book. Now the Second Creation is as complex, if not more complex, than the first one. The first question that I had for the Lord in understanding this Second Creation was: "Why are there so many differences between the first two chapters of Genesis?" I notice that the order of creation in the first Chapter was different from the creation in the second Chapter of Genesis.

Chapter Three

THE CREATION OF THE SPIRIT MAN

I t is time to see what God did on the sixth day of the second creation. As we study this creation, there will be key secrets that you must study closely, so that you will not miss what that creation consists of. In the Second Creation of God, I asked the Holy Spirit to teach me about this creation, because it was more complex to understand without the **secrets** that are in the word of God. In the Second Creation of God, there are many things listed about it that are different from the creation many of us think it is. As I read the first Chapter of Genesis, I found things that I had never thought of before. I saw things that I had never seen before. The Holy Spirit showed me that it was in this Second Creation that the sun, moon, and stars were created, therefore God placed them where He wanted them to be. That part I understood, but I had another problem in understanding one thing: How could the creation of the earthly man be in that same duration of time, since the earth was eon years old? Come with me to see how the Holy Spirit has showed me **many secrets** that helped me to understand the Second Creation of God. This is the third time the word "creation" was used, in Genesis 1:27. It was God's timing to create the spiritual man in this second creation.

I could see all of the great sea creatures' move back and forth in the waters. What a sight it was. It was good to see where all of the creatures came from as I watched. God had a different plan for this creation. **First**, God renewed the earth with everything needed for His newly created family that was going to be created or made. The waters were back in place, and all of the firmaments were divided. The earth brought forth trees, herbs, grass, and fruit trees. The waters were filled with great sea creatures and fish. Every living creature was moving on the earth. Now God was ready to create a man in His own image. The First Creation was the testing ground for the angels and Lucifer. The Second Creation is going to be the testing ground for the spiritual beings that God created.

A conversation took place in the council of the Godhead in the heavenly realm, right after God renewed the whole earth. **Genesis 1:26, "Then God said, 'Let Us make man in Our image'"** God created a man in His own image. In these two verses there is no mention of God taking any of the dust of the earth to make this man. Nor did God take a rib out of this spirit man to make the female in these two verses. Does this sound strange to you? There are many strange things that happened in this second creation of God that are different from the next chapter, which shows that there are two different creations. Everything that is created in both of these are created or made in different time frames.

Look at *Genesis 1:27, "So God created* **man** *in His own image; in the image of God created* **him;** **male** *and* **female** *He created them*.**" Old Testament prophets wrote the scriptures as they were led by the Holy Spirit of God. Some of the scriptures were written in secret codes or key verses, in a fashion so that the ordinary person could not understand their meaning, but only God's chosen ones could understand them. Jesus always spoke in parables when He was here on the earth, so that the foolish ones could not understand what He was saying. Even His disciples were not able to understand them, so they asked Him for the understanding of their meaning. God needed someone to be in charge of this second creation on the earth whom

He could trust, who was made in His own image. God had a conversation with the Son and the Holy Spirit, saying, "**Let Us** *make man in* **Our** *image, according to* **Our** *likeness.*" I knew that this was going to be exciting for me to watch the Creator making man in His own image. God was about to make a man in His own image; **this man was not made from the dust of the earth in this second creation**. God's image was not flesh, for God is a Spirit. God was going to make a male and a female spirit; just like Himself. He made them in His very image, in His likeness. I noticed that **God did not take any dust from the earth at this time** "*(vs. 27) So* **God created man in His own image;** *in the* **image** *of* **God He created him**; *male and female He created them.*" He created them at the same time in (vs. 27). Please notice in the first part of this verse that "man" was created in God's image. What is the image of God? The Godhead consist of three parts: God the Father, God the Son, and God the Holy Spirit.

I want to talk about the image of God, so I need to explain a few things about this subject first before I talk about the spiritual man. God created this spirit man in three parts, just like Himself. There is a spiritual body, soul, and spirit. This subject is hard to explain in human terms – actually it is impossible – because the human mind cannot understand the things of God.

2 Corinthians 5:1-9, **(vs. 1) For we know that if our earthly house, this tent, is destroyed, we have a building from God, a house not made with hands, eternal in the heavens. (vs. 2) for in this we groan, earnestly desiring to be clothed with our habitation which is from heaven,**

The tent refers to our earthly body. Paul says that if it is destroyed, we have a building from God, an eternal house in heaven. God has a spiritual body made by Him, which is the eternal house in heaven. Therefore it is made for you. You see, the earthly body that our spirit was put into was not the permanent dwelling for our spirit. In the beginning of time, before man was formed, God created man's spirit in the image of Himself. Man was made of spirit, soul, and body, and we were made in God's image, what is known as the spirit man. Before the spirit entered our earthly body, it already had a soul and a spiritual body. The life-source of each one of us is our spirit, therefore the body without this spirit is dead. **The earthly body cannot live without the spirit, but the spirit can live and is alive without the earthly body!** The moment that your body gives up the spirit, your earthly body dies, <u>for the absence of spirit means the absence of</u>

life. Life comes from the spirit joining the flesh. The spirit that is in you is the real you. The flesh is just your outer covering, a tent.

The (vs. 1) **building from God, a house not made with hands, eternal in the heavens.** Is our spiritual outer covering for the spiritual soul and spirit that each one of us has? Before our fleshly man was ever formed by God, our spirit man was already created in the second creation. This subject was mentioned already in this book, but we must look at it again because it is important to discuss this, so that you can understand its meaning.

We are naked without the heavenly body that belongs to us. The heavenly body is made up of non-perishable material that will last forever. It is being reserved for us in heaven till we get there. The Bible tells us that God knew us before we were in our mother's womb. We know that our spirit belongs to God and must go back to Him when we die, for the body without the spirit is dead. In this scripture, God created both male and female.

He made both in His image, which was spirit, soul and body. Now keep in mind that there is a spirit body that is made of a different material than our earthly body. The spirit body cannot be destroyed, therefore it will last forever. The fleshly body, which is made of the earth, will not last forever until it is resurrected when the dead in Christ are raised from the dead. Your spirit is the real you, not the outer flesh. The outer part of your flesh is just a temporary shell, covering your spirit and soul.

Genesis 5:1, 2, (vs. 1) "This is the book of the genealogy of Adam. In the day that <u>God created man,</u> He made him in the likeness of God. (vs. 2) <u>He created them male and female</u>, and blessed them and called them Mankind in the day they were created.

I find this interesting, because this refers to Genesis 1:27, and because man was created, not formed him. They both were called man. (*Genesis 1:27, "So God created man in His own image, in the image of God. He created him; male and female He created them."*)

Point 1. God created man in the second creation in His likeness. God was not made of human flesh, but Spirit, which consists of three Spirit beings: God the Father, the Son, and the Holy Spirit. These three are one. So in this creation, God created a spiritual man in His image, made of spiritual substance. "*He created* **him***; **male** and **female** *He created them.*"

There are three parts of this spiritual man God created: First, God created him. This "him" was the spiritual house of the next two parts. Male and female were created next to go inside of the spiritual housing of the "him." I know that this is hard for you to understand, because it was hard for me, too. But when the earthly man was formed, he had the three parts living inside of him too: the body, soul, and spirit.

Point 2. The Second creation I am talking about is all about the spiritual man that was created. Because in this creation the sun was created, which is older than 6,000 years. So the earthly man that was created could not have been created in this second creation of God. I know that what I am writing here is very controversial, and it took me a long time to understand these scriptures. I believe firmly in the word of God, the Holy Spirit, and Jesus the Son of God.

The word of God can only be understood by your spiritual man, through the Holy Spirit's teaching. The Godhead is very hard to understand. Just take a look around to see how many denominations there are. Almost everyone has a different opinion about the trinity. I am just an ordinary man, who only has a high school education, but that does not matter. Why? Because, I have a teacher who created the universe, therefore that qualifies me to be able to write whatever He instructs me to write. Is God three persons that are alike, or three persons in one being?

Jesus said unto the disciples, "If you have seen Me, you have seen the Father." Another question I might ask: "How can Christ be in every believer at the same time? Is there more than one?" I do not want to confuse you, I just want you to see that it is important for you to be open to the teaching of the Word of God with your mind and with your spirit. God is a Spirit, which is the **spiritual dwelling** of the Holy Spirit **and** the Son of God. In the spiritual realm, things are different from in the earthly realm, for in the spiritual realm there are no limitations. There is no sickness, no death or darkness, for they need no sleep, nor do they get tired. God the Father, and the Son, works with the Holy Spirit together as one. Look at the creation: God spoke the Word, saying: "Let there be light, and there was light." The Holy Spirit was moving over the face of the waters. When He heard the spoken word, He moved to perform the task. Jesus is the Word. In Him there is life. All three are working together. God spoke the Word, which was Jesus, in whom all of creation was made. The Holy Spirit obeyed, causing the work to be done.

Now I will explain the second part of the verse: *(vs. 1: 27)* "in the **image** *of* **God He created him**; *male and female He created them.*" In heaven things are very different from on the earth. In heaven there are no limitations to what the angels or spirits can do. They can feel no pain, nor do they get sick. They can be visible or invisible. They can be fruitful and multiply, as you will see in the next verse.

Look closely, then you will see the three parts. First He created "man." This is the spiritual house of the next two parts. The second part was "male" or the "spirit" part. The third part was the "female" or the soul part of the spiritual housing. Spirit, soul, and body, all three in one being, just like God. The Godhead has the three parts: the Father, Son, and Holy Spirit. They are all in one Spirit being, yet they operate in three manifestations with the same purpose in mind. They operate as three, yet they move together as one. The Father is in the Son, and the Son is in the Father as well as the Holy Spirit. *John 8:42, "Jesus said to them, If God were your Father, you would love Me, for* **I proceeded forth and came from God**; *nor have I come of Myself, but* **He sent Me**.*"* Jesus, the Son of God, came from His Father, as we can see from this scripture. All three of the trinity live inside each other.

Just a note to add to those thoughts. The Second Creation was created by God, so that He could create for us a spiritual man, made in the image of God, to be a covering of our spirit and soul. The spirit plus the soul were referred to as the male and female in

Genesis 1:27. They had the power to reproduce by multiplying to fill the earth, in this second creation of God. As you can see, this is a hard subject for anyone to understand in the natural state of mind, but in the spiritual state of the mind, it can be understood.

Let us make man in our image. Can you see it yet? A spiritual body, soul, and spirit made of a non-flesh substance in the likeness of God. He created both male and female in one being, and *He called them "man."* He then told them to be fruitful and multiply. They could do that because they were created in His image. The earth during this duration was filled with these spiritual creations. How many, we will never know. Were there other human life forms living then? There were all of the created animals, birds, living creatures, fish and other ocean creatures. We know that Lucifer's kingdom on the earth was destroyed, but he and the other fallen angels were not destroyed. Spirit men can eat food the same way we do. They can be invisible or made to be visible. Take Jesus, for instance. When He arose from the dead, He was seen by many of His disciples on several occasions. He ate fish and drank beverages also. He walked through walls, and He appeared and disappeared at His will (John 20:19, 21:12). The spirit male and female were able to reproduce themselves to fill the earth. I was not told much else about this created earth, in this first chapter of Genesis.

What is the image of God? When you stand in front of a mirror, what image do you see in that mirror? When I look in the mirror, I see an image that looks like me. Sometimes I do not like what I see, but the only way for me to change the image I see is to change my own appearance, then the image in that mirror will change into the same image as me.

Genesis 1:26, (vs. 26) "Then God said, 'Let Us make man in Our image, according to Our likeness; let them have the dominion over the fish of the sea, over the birds of the air, and over the cattle, over all the earth and over every creeping thing that creeps on the earth.' (vs. 27) So God created man in His own image; in the image of God created him; male and female He created them."

So God created a **man** who looked just like Himself. So now, I must take you deeper into this verse. The Godhead is three in one, the Father, the Son, and the Holy Spirit. For this man that God created to look like Himself, this spirit man must be created as three in one also. How can I say that? There are words in this verse that show there are three distinct beings being made in one spirit being. The Second Creation is all about the spiritual man that God created. It will take time for me to explain what this spirit man is made of. I have already told you some things, but I am sure that it was not enough to explain what this spiritual man consists of. First of all, I am sure that you know what you are made up of. You are made up of a body, soul, and spirit; these three parts are what you really consist of. With that in mind, by the same token, the spiritual man consists of three parts also. This is how God created all of us.

So now I will try to explain in detail what the spirit man, which God created, consists of. I will be giving you secret key words from the two scriptures you just read. (Vs. 26), "**Then God said, 'Let Us make man in Our image, according to Our likeness."** God was telling us, that He, along with the Holy Spirit and His Son, was going to make a man in their image and likeness. God did not make the man by Himself. He worked with the Son and the Holy Spirit to accomplish the task of making a spirit man. **"Let Us"** refers to the other two parts of the Godhead.

In all of God's creations, God uses His Son plus the Holy Spirit to get the job finished. God speaks the "word," which is the Son (Jesus), the Holy Spirit moves over the object or substance, then the thing the Father speaks out of His mouth comes into being.

God creates the spirit man for a purpose, because in the next part of the verse, God told us what His purpose was for the spirit man: (vs. 26), "**let them have dominion over the fish of the sea, over the birds of the air, and over the cattle, over all the earth and over every creeping thing that creeps on the earth.**" After God renewed the earth, He had a plan for this new earth to fulfill. It was to be controlled or ruled by the spirit man that God created. *Genesis 1:27,* *"So God created* **man** *in His own image; in the image of God created* **him; male** *and* **female** *He created them.*" Here comes the hard part for me, to explain how or what the spirit man is made up of. There are key secret words in this verse that will unlock this mystery. Actually, in (vs. 27), God does explain what the three parts of the spirit man He created consist of: **"him;** (the spirit man) **male** *and* **female."** First God created the spirit **"man"** to be a spiritual being like Himself, because God is a Spirit; He is not flesh, but Spirit. Then at the same time, God created the other two parts of the spirit **"man"** so that he would be like Him. God created **"him;** (the spirit man) **male** *and* **female."** The spirit **"man"** had two other parts within himself (**male** *and* **female**) just like his Creator had. The **"spirit man"** was the spiritual house (dwelling place) for the **male** *and* **female** spirit beings. He is made up of three: the spiritual **body**, the spiritual **soul**, and the spirit; body, soul, spirit. This can be confusing. It sure was for me. We all believe that we are made up of three parts also: we are body, soul, and spirit. You cannot see your other two parts, can you? No. So why can you not understand about the things I just talked about? God says something in the next verse that might be confusing also.

Genesis 1:27, "So God created **man** *in His own image; in the image of God created* **him; male** *and* **female** *He created them."* (A paraphrase example of this verse in my own words would read: So God created a spiritual man in His image; He did not create him as a single being, but created him as a three-in-one being, like Himself, within the spirit man; God also create male and female spirit beings in him, which makes him a spiritual man with three parts; celestial body, soul, spirit.)

God created the man to be just like Him, so this man God created was a spirit man made just like Him, who is a Spirit also. The man God created was created as three persons in one body, like God. The man God created had a body that was made of a spiritual substance that was a celestial body like its Creator. Within this celestial body was a soul or male part. Within that same body was a spirit or the female part. Thus, we have all three parts of the spiritual man. The male was Adam's spirit and the female was Eve's spirit. In this Second Creation of God, their spirits were in the spirit man created, so the three became one, way before the creation of the fleshly man and woman, who were formed from the dust of the earth in the next creation, which is the third creation where we now live. I will talk about them in the next chapter.

May I take you a little deeper, so that you can understand what I have been saying so far? There is only one God, yet He has two other parts that are in Him: the Son, and the Holy Spirit, they are all one. The Godhead is sometimes hard for us to understand. How can they live inside each other, yet operate outside of each other? How can Jesus be on the earth, yet He is in the Father at the same time? Our little minds cannot understand these things in our natural way of thinking. Yes, if we let the Holy Spirit teach us through our spiritual man that is on the inside of us, then truly it is possible to understand the things of God. In the spiritual realm, things are different from the natural realm. In the natural realm, the earthly man has three parts. He has a natural body, he has a spirit within himself that is eternal, and he also has a soul, which is eternal. The spirit and the soul within the man are what make the earthly body stay alive. If the spirit and soul leave the earthly man, he will die. So the earthly man has these limitations while here on the earth. They all three work together within the realm of the earthly man, until they are called out of the earthly being.

The earthly man brought on himself the sentence of death to his earthly shell when he sinned against God. That is why he now has these limitations. He has become a man who has two other parts of his being that are eternal, but the main part, which is his body, must return to dust he was created from when he dies. But the other two parts (soul and the spirit) go back to God to be judged.

Now the spirit man that God created was created to last forever, along with the male and female spirits. All three spirit beings are eternal beings forever. They are all three in one being, yet they have no limitations on themselves. They can move as one or they can operate separately outside of that one body. No matter what function they operate in, they still move as one, even if they operate outside of themselves. They were created in God's image and likeness, so they can move as He moves.

Can I take you a little deeper with me? The Godhead, the Father, the Son, and the Holy Spirit are one, yet they operate as three. They work together as one, yet as three. In Genesis 1:1-3, the Spirit of God was hovering over the water, then God spoke and said, "Let there be light," and the light appeared, which the Son of God is. The three of them worked as three, yet they are one. Each part of the Godhead can move as three separate beings outside of themselves, just like in Genesis when they performed as three separate beings, but with one purpose. Now the spirit man that God created works the same way, because the three of them are one also, but can work as three as well. Remember, all three of them have no limitations either. Plus they are created eternal. Now with all of these facts in mind, I hope that you can see how the spirit man can multiply as God commanded the spirit man's male and female parts to do. He said for them to be fruitful and multiply. Also He told them to fill the earth. In the spiritual world, there are things done that we humans cannot understand for sure. The spirit man that God created is not like the human body that we have, because the three parts of our beings are limited in what they can do. But the spiritual being that God created is not limited to what it can do because it is made of non-perishable substance. Every part of its being can operate in the supernatural to whatever God directs it to do.

Genesis 1:28, "Then God blessed them, and God said to them, 'Be fruitful and multiply; fill the earth and subdue it; have dominion over the fish of the sea, over the birds of the air, and over every living thing that moves on the earth.'"

In this second creation, God did not give the **"man"** a name. God could have named him, but He chose not to do that. Now in (vs. 28), God blessed them. Who is "them"? It was the **male** and **female** part of the **"man."** The whole spiritual **"man"** was created three in one, just like its Creator. God gave the inner part of the **"man"** a command. He told them, the **male** *and* **female** part of the **"man"** to: **"Be fruitful and multiply."** That might sound strange to you, because in your mind you were taught that this referred to Adam and Eve in the next chapter. But this is not true, because I have already showed you the reason why. So these verses belong to the second creation, because God is creating the spiritual **"man"** in this creation, which will be the spiritual part of Adam and Eve in the next creation.

How can the spirit **"man"** be able to produce other spiritual beings? The spirit **"man"** has everything within himself to be able to do this. He has the **male** *and* **female** parts in himself that are able to reproduce themselves. God talked to the **male** (**Adam's spirit**) and female (**Eve's spirit**) part of the **"man"** and said to them: **"Be fruitful and multiply."** By God saying that to them, it is established that they are able to do the thing God commanded them to do: they were able to produce other spirit beings. The command of God became greater in the next part of the verse, for He said to them: **"fill the earth and subdue it; have dominion over the fish of the sea, over the birds of the air, and over every living thing that moves on the earth."** Again, this command of God was for the spirit **"man"** to accomplish first. Then in the next chapter the spiritual male and female were breathed into the earthly beings of Adam and Eve. What happened in this second creation of God? There is not a lot of scripture telling us exactly what happened, but there are some hidden secrets, telling us that there were a lot of things going on then. This second creation of God was for the spiritual beings to fill the earth. It is not known for sure how long this creation lasted, but it did last for a long time because it was in this creation that the sun, moon, and the stars were created. One thing for sure, the **male** *and* **female** parts of the spirit **"man"** did what God commanded them to do. Everything on the earth was perfect, especially because Lucifer did not have control of the earth at that time, because God gave the spirit **"man"** power over the earth. Mainly this is because God renewed the earth this time, so that

He could test the spiritual males and females to see if they would remain faithful to Him.

May I remind you of an important thing that took place in this creation? In this Second Creation of God, God created or made everything on the earth before He created the spirit male and female. But in the next creation in Chapter Two, the earthly man was formed out of the dust before everything else was made out of the earth. I do not have a lot of information about this Second Creation, I only have a few scriptures on it, but with the help of the Holy Spirit, you and I can receive understanding on this subject. As far as the age of the sun, moon or stars, I know in our modern times they are very old indeed, so with that being said, I know that the earthly man Adam could not have been born in that duration of time. That is why I believe that there are three creations of the earth in the first two chapters of Genesis.

I heard God speak again: *Genesis 1:29-31, (29) "And God said, 'See, I have given you every herb that yields seed which is on the face of all the earth, and every tree whose fruit yields seed; to you it shall be for food. (30) Also, to every **beast** of the earth, to every bird of the air, and to everything that creeps on the earth, in which there is life, I have given every green herb for food'; and it was so. (31) Then God saw everything* *that He had made, and indeed it was very good. So the evening and the morning were the* **sixth day.***"*

Please read **Genesis 2:1: "thus the heavens and the earth, and all the host of them, were finished."** It was in that creation that all that work was done in seven days. In this Second Creation, everything was created by the spoken word in the first six days, until God created man in His own image. He created male and female. He blessed them and said for them to be fruitful and multiply. In this creation, they were not made of earthly material, they were created, not formed of the dust of the earth. God created the Second Creation for one purpose, so that everyone who was ever to be born on the earth could have a spirit to be placed in them, so that they could live, because without a spirit there could be no life. I was not told how long this took place, so it could have been eon of years. There is no scripture in the Bible stating how long it remained in that state. Before I tell you how this Second Creation ended, I want to show you that in the word of God, angels can produce children when they leave their own place and come together with humanity. This is why I have added an extra chapter in this book, so that I could show you what happened in Genesis.

Chapter Four

"SONS OF GOD" AND GIANTS IN THE LAND

Genesis 6:1-4 *"(vs. 1) Now it came to pass, when men began to multiply on the face of the earth, and daughters were born unto them, (vs. 2) that the* **sons of God saw the daughters of men, that they were beautiful; and they took them wives for themselves of all whom they chose**. *(vs. 3) And the Lord said, My spirit shall not strive with man forever, for he is indeed flesh; yet his days shall be one hundred and twenty years. (vs. 4) There* **were giants in the earth in those days**; *and* **also after that**, *when the* **sons of God came in to the daughters of men and they bare children to them,** *those where the mighty men who were of old, men of renown." (NIV)*

The serpent (Satan) already showed up in Genesis 3. Now his followers, which are fallen angels, came on the scene in these scriptures above. The sons of God are mentioned many times in the Bible. All angels, whether good or bad, are called sons of God. I, too, wanted to know how angels could produce children. After all, the Second Creation that I talked about was a creation of spirit beings, which were to multiply and fill the earth. So this, my friend, is the reason for this chapter on fallen angels, the sons of God.

I always thought angels were mostly invisible, but these scriptures prove that they can be very visible. They can become tangible by interacting with humans at their will. The first time I read these scriptures, it almost blew me away. I thought, "How can angels have sexual relations with humans?" But clearly, they did: "*when the* **sons of God came in unto the daughters of men, and they bare children to them,** *the same became mighty men which were of old, men of renown." (6:4).* by them doing that, they produced: *"(vs. 4) There* **were giants in the earth in those days***;"* as you can clearly see in this verse.

There is a **key secret** right in the middle of (vs. 4); "**also after that**" -- not only were there giants before the flood of Noah, Moses also said even after that, there would be giants. It is easy to skip over those three little words, but those three little words have deep meaning: there would be other giants later. The sons of God in these scriptures are those angels who fell with Lucifer in the first creation of God. Because of their evil deeds, God was not pleased with man, for He said:

Genesis 6:5-7 (vs. 5) "Then the Lord saw that the wickedness of man was great in the earth, and that every intent of the thoughts of his heart was only evil continually. (vs. 6) And the Lord was sorry the He had made man on the earth, and He was grieved in His heart. (vs. 7) So the Lord said, 'I will destroy man whom I have cre- ated from the face of the earth, both man and the beast, creeping thing and birds of the air, for I am sorry that I have made them.'"

Here it is again, that serpent and his angel followers caused man to sin again, which caused God to want to destroy the earth again. Every time that Satan has control of the earth, he causes God to destroy it. I will show you that there are two classes of fallen angels in the next few verses. There are the fallen angels who are loose with Satan, then there are angels who left their own place and committed greater sins with the human race. "*(vs. 2) that the* **sons of God saw the daughters of men, that they were beautiful;**

and they took them wives for themselves of all whom they chose." Look at what brother Jude said about these fallen angels: *Jude 6, 7 "(vs. 6) And* **the angels** *who* **did not keep their proper domain**, *but* **left their own abode. He has reserved in everlasting chains under darkness** *for the* **judgment** *of the* **great day***; (vs.7) as Sodom and Gomorrah, and the cities around them in a similar manner to these,* **having given themselves over to sexual flesh**, *are set forth as an example,* **suffering the vengeance of eternal fire**." The angels who committed the sexual crimes were "**reserved in everlasting chains under darkness** *for the* **judgment** *of the* **great day**." It is not clear when God did this, but Jude said that it happened. The reason I am bringing these things up about the angels is that if they can have sexual contact with humans, then what I said about the second creation is true. However, they did not have contact with the humans, but only with each other. The angels Jude is talking about are the angels in Genesis 6:2.

The giants are the product of the angels and the human race. Peter was aware of those fallen angels also in the New Testament. Both Peter and Jude wrote about these fallen angels, therefore I want to show you those scriptures as you and I travel on this journey through time.

1 Peter 3:18-20, "(vs.18) For Christ also suffered once for sins, the just for the unjust, that He might bring us to God, being put to death in the flesh but made alive by the Spirit, (vs. 19) by whom also **He went and preached to the spirits in prison, (vs. 20) who formerly were disobedient,** *when once the* **Divine longsuffering waited in the days of Noah,** *while the ark was being prepared, in the which a few, that is, eight souls, were saved through water."* When Christ was crucified, He went and preached to those spirits (the fallen angels who had sex during the time of Noah) in prison. He may have preached also to the spirits of those who refused to hear Noah's preaching, which lasted 120 years. God waited all that time for those people to repent from their evil deeds.

1 Peter 4:1-6, "(Vs. 1) Therefore, since Christ suffered for us in the flesh, arm yourselves also with the same mind, for he who has suffered in the flesh has ceased from sin, (vs. 2) that he no longer should live the rest of his time in the flesh for the lust of men, but for the will of God. (v. 3) For we have spent enough of our past lifetime in doing the will of the Gentiles - when we walked in lewdness, lust, drunkenness, revelries, drinking parties, and abominable idolatries. (vs.4) In regard to these, they think it strange that you do not run with them in the same flood of dissipation, speaking evil of you. (vs. 5) They will give an account to Him who is ready to judge the living and the dead. (vs. 6) **For this reason the gospel was preached also to those who are dead,** *that they might be judged according to men in the flesh, but live according to God in the spirit."*

I believe that when Christ preached down in this prison to all those who were spiritually dead, He preached unto them that they would be judged according to the flesh, because they lived in the flesh, not in the spirit. Then the last part of that verse, *"but live according to God in the spirit,"* was a sermon for the ones who lived in paradise, because those who live according to the Spirit shall not be judged according to the flesh. *2 Peter 2:4,5 "(vs. 4) For if* **God did not spare the angels who sinned,** *but* **cast them down to hell and delivered them into chains of darkness,** *to be reserved for judgment; (vs.5) and did not spare the ancient world, but saved Noah, one of the eight people, a preacher of righteousness, bringing the flood on the world of the ungodly; (vs. 9) then the Lord knows how to deliver the godly out of temptations and to reserve the unjust under punishment for that day of judgment."* There are giants mentioned in several books of the Bible, the products of fallen angels having sexual relationships with the human race. Primarily they did those practices in places where the lineage of Christ was to exist. The giants were a tool of Satan, to try to stop the seed of the woman producing the seed in Jesus' lineage. Satan was almost successful in defeating God's plan before the third flood, but did not succeed because God saved eight people in the ark. The reason God destroyed everything, including the children in the flood, was to destroy all of the giants among them that defiled the human race. But Satan sent some of his angels to start more giants after the flood of Noah, knowing that God made a promise not to destroy the earth with water again. He now had a better chance to try to stop the seed of the woman producing Christ's lineage. But God was not done yet. He told Israel to destroy all of the giants. David and his servants destroyed the last of them.

THE LAST OF THE GIANTS DESTROYED

David already killed the strongest giant, Goliath, in 1 Samuel 17:48-51. Now it was time to kill the rest of the giants. As far as I know, these five giants were the last ones on the earth.

2 Samuel 21:15-22, "(vs. 15) When the Philistines were at war again with Israel, David and his servants with him went down and fought the Philistines; and David grew faint. (vs. 16) Then **Ishbi-Benob***, who was* **one of the sons of the giant***, the weight of whose bronze spear was three hundred shekels, who was bearing a new sword, thought he could kill David. (vs. 17) But* **Abishai** *the son of Zeruiah* **came to his aid, and struck the Philistine and killed him.** *Then the men of David swore to him, saying, 'You shall go out no more with us to battle, lest you quench the lamp of Israel.'" (vs. 18) Now it hap-pened afterward that there was again a battle with the Philistines at Gob. Then* **Sibbechai** *the Hushathite* **killed Saph***, who was* **one of the sons of the giant***. (vs. 19) Again there was war at Gob, with the Philistines, where* **Elhanan** *the son of Jaare-Oregim the Bethlehemite* **killed the brother of Goliath** *the Gittite, the shaft of whose spear was like a weaver's beam. (vs. 20) Yet again there was war at Gath, where there was a* **man of great stature***, who had six fin-gers on each hand and six toes on each foot, twenty-four in number, and* **he also was born to the giant***. (vs. 21) So when he defied Israel,* **Jonathan** *the son of Shimea, David's brother,* **killed him***. (vs., 22) These four were born to* *the giant in Gath, and fell by the hand of David and by the hand of his servants."*

Counting Goliath, plus these four giants, that gives us a total of five giants that were killed by David and his servants. I believe it was after this God put an end of the angels who left their first estate, when Peter said these things: *2 Peter 2:4,5 "(vs. 4) For if* **God did not spare the angels who sinned**, *but* **cast them down to hell and delivered them into chains of darkness**, *to be reserved for judgment."* Satan's last attempt to stop God's plan will be during the great Tribulation and after he is released after the one thousand-year reign of Christ. It is then he will be cast into the lake of fire forever.

Chapter Five

THE SECOND FLOOD "THE END OF THE SECOND CREATION"

The **seventh** day was a very restful day for me, as well as for God. Everything that God made was good and perfect, so **God created the seventh day for rest**. *Genesis 2:1, "Thus the heavens and the earth, and all the host of them, were finished. (vs. 2) And on the seventh day God ended His work which He had done, and He rested on the seventh day from all His work which He had done. (vs. 3) Then God blessed the seventh day and sanctified it, because in it He rested from all His work which God had created and made."*

This is the end of the Second Creation of God. I was not told how long it lasted, but I am sure it lasted a long time because of the age of the earth. The seventh day was an important day to God, important enough to bless it and sanctify it. It seemed like I was on the earth a long time in this Second Creation of God, so I am glad that I was on this imaginary trip, because I would be eon of years old by now. I was now getting ready to take another voyage into the dimension of the Third Creation of God, where I used to live. But first I needed to see how the Second Creation ended. I also needed to know how it was destroyed.

Peter saw something in *2 Peter 3:3-7: "(vs. 3.) Knowing this first: that scoffers will come in the last days, walking according to their <u>own lust</u>, (vs. 4.) and saying, 'Where is the promise of His coming? For since the fathers fell asleep, all things continue as they were <u>from the beginning of creation.</u>' (vs. 5.) For this they willfully forget: <u>that</u> **by the word of God** <u>the</u> **heavens were of old,** *and the* **earth standing out of water** *and* **in the** *water,* (vs. 6.) *by which the* **world that then existed perished,** *being flooded with water.* (vs. 7.)* But th**e** **heavens and the earth which are now pre-served by the same word**, *are reserved for fire until the Day of Judgment and perdition of ungodly men."*

Peter gives us a little insight as to how the Second Creation ended by hiding secret keys in the fifth verse. *"(vs. 5.) For this they willfully forget: <u>that</u> **by the word of God** <u>the</u> **heavens were of old,** *and the* **earth**

standing out of water *and* **in the water,** *(vs. 6.) by* *which the* **world that then existed perished,** *being* *flooded with water."*

Many people think that Peter is referring to the flood of Noah. In Noah's flood, the whole earth did not perish. God spared Noah and his family, plus two of every living thing. The **secret** is in his descriptions. First Peter was saying, way back in time, before our creation the: **heavens were of old,** I saw the **earth standing out of water** after the first creation, for a period of time, but in his next breath the earth was back: **in the water.** Then Peter saw a world system being destroyed in his next breath: "*(vs. 6.) by which the* **world that then existed perished,** *being flooded with water."* Everything was destroyed on the earth except the things in the waters. Peter saw the second flood, which ended the Second Creation of God. It was as if Peter was saying these things in a parable, like Jesus did, so that the wise of the world would miss its real meaning. The words in (vs. 5, 6) run together in a way that they could cause confusion or misunderstanding. Now in the second part of (vs. 5) and (vs. 6), a change took place for the earth, in which Peter saw by revelation of the Spirit that the earth was covered in water, because "*the* **world that then existed perished,** *being flooded with water."* Peter saw the second creation of Genesis 1:2-2:3 being destroyed by water in (vs. 6). He said that the world that then existed perished. Nothing was left except the earth itself.

I read these scriptures many times before with the understanding that Peter was just talking about the flood of Noah. But the Holy Spirit taught me some very important lessons when I asked Him to give me understanding on the subject of God's creations. In Noah's flood, the whole world did not perish. The trees survived, the grass, the herbs, as a matter fact, nowhere in that text did God have to renew the earth again. First, Peter was saying that the earth was not covered by water in the beginning of the second creation. He also said that the heavens were very old. Both of them were created by the spoken Word of God. When you read these scriptures with your natural way of thinking and think with your natural mind, you will miss the full impact of what Peter is saying. I have read these scriptures many times before, thinking that he was just talking about the flood in Noah's time.

But now, I read it with a different understanding, because the Holy Spirit has taught me how to study by listening to His voice, instead of listening to my own understanding. God has hidden the meaning of the scriptures from the world, but reveals its meaning to His children. **In these verses, there is a hidden**

treasure of understanding that must be unlocked, so that you can understand the true revelation of the creation of the heavens and the earth. After I had studied these scriptures very carefully, by the inspiration of the Holy Spirit, the meaning of 2 Peter 3:3-7 came to life in my spirit. It was clear to me now that Peter was talking about the second creation of God instead of Noah's flood. Like I said, it took me a while before I could see the comparison of the verses between the Old and New Testaments. Moses was the Old Testament preacher and Peter was the New Testament preacher. They were far apart in years, yet they were close by the Holy Spirit in their teaching.

I know that it is hard to believe, but with the Holy Spirit's help, you will be able to understand these scriptures. In the first part of this (vs. 5) the earth was standing out of the water before it was covered with the flood waters. We have come to the end of the Second Creation of God, when it was flooded with water once again, for this was the second time that God flooded the earth. You and I have covered a lot of different views on the first two creations of God so far. We have yet three more to cover. I do not have enough scripture or insight on those two creations, only what I have shared with you so far to really know for sure what took place in those creations. Believe me, it was hard enough for me to understand what has been written so far.

We may never know all of the details, but I am sure that our little minds could not even begin to understand them. Hold on to your seat belts, for you are about to go on another trip with me into the Third Creation of God. Before we go there, I want to go over a few things that I have covered about the first two creations of God. In the First Creation, Genesis 1:1, when Noah said, "*In the beginning God created the heavens and the earth,*" "*In the beginning*" refers to the earth and the heavens' beginning! Not God's beginning, because God is eternal. He has no beginning or ending of time! So their beginning could have been million of years ago.

Let me show you how it would read in my own paraphrase version: "Many years ago, God, created the heavens and the earth, but now I want to show you what happened to it since then. I was not given the reason why it was void and covered with water; but I was shown how God re-created it in this Second Creation. Look how the First Creation ended, it had no distinct form, and it became full of darkness. I will now show you what God did to it in this Second Creation." In the beginning of the creation of the heavens and the earth, God would not have created them in the fashion stated in (vs. 2). God never creates things that are messed up. These facts suggest that Noah is talking about two different creations. The First Creation I talked about was easy enough to understand, because I have heard that there was a gap between the first two verses in Genesis 1. But I never heard what could have been on it at that time, until I received knowledge from the Holy Spirit.

Now the Second Creation was much harder for me to understand, because I was taught that it was the creation where Adam and Eve were created. But I was not satisfied with that answer because the age factor of the earth did not match what we now know about the age of the earth. The Second Creation of God that we are now leaving behind, to go to the Third Creation of God, was a creation a little like the first, with the exception of a few things. The first had everything in it except the sun, stars, and moon, as we have discussed already. It also had animals. It had Lucifer in charge of it until his rebellion. The Second Creation had new tenants to take care of it, who were spiritual beings, but God created the sun, moon, and stars in this creation. He gave His newly created spirit, male and female, to be in charge of everything that was on the earth that God created. There is another gap between Genesis 2:3 and 2:4, because it is the place we will find the Third Creation, the place we all live in now. I have never heard about this gap theory in my sixty-two years that I have been on this earth. Now for me, this one was hard for me to understand. I had to rely on the Holy Spirit as He taught me these things. Come with me as the Holy Spirit and I go into the realm of the Third Creation of God.

Here is a brief summary of what took place and what is to come.

The First Creation did not need the sun, moon or stars, because God provided the light. The last creation will not have the sun, either. I find that interesting -- how about you? All of the rest of God's creations have the sun, moon, and stars in them. Another interesting thing is that the **first creation** was created to test the angels of God. The **Second Creation** of God was to test the spiritual beings God created. The **Third Creation** was to test the earthly man and woman to see if they could remain faithful to Him. The **Fourth Creation** will be the testing ground for the saints of God who did not take the mark of the beast and the whole house of Israel, in the new earthly Jerusalem, during and after the thousand-year reign. In the first part of the Fourth Creation, Satan is bound for 1,000 years. Then Satan will be loosed after the thousand-year reign to tempt or test those nations. Finally, in the **Fifth** and last **Creation** of God, God finally has the earth made perfect, with perfect saints. Plus Satan could not ever appear again. God brings the New Jerusalem down from heaven to the earth, to make the earth heaven on earth.

All of these creations were not mistakes of God. No, not at all. They were created so that all of God's created beings could have free will to choose right or wrong, to choose to serve God or not to serve God. God chose not to create robots. He wanted to create beings of choice. He wanted His creations to be in His kingdom, because they accepted His invitation to become His sons or daughters by asking Jesus to be the Lord of their lives.

{Just a note: God our Father knew exactly how many spiritual male and female spirits He needed to create in the second creation. That is probably why that creation lasted so long. Every human that is born in this third creation has to have a spirit to live. So God made enough of them in the second creation to fulfill that need. I know now that in the Second Creation, God created Adam and Eve's spirit, therefore every other spirit was produced through them.}

Genesis 1:28, "Then God blessed them, and God said to them, 'Be fruitful and multiply; fill the earth and subdue it.'"

Chapter Six

ENTERING THE THIRD CREATION OF GOD

I was not sure how long I floated on the earth at the end of the Second Creation of God, but when I finally rested on dry ground, I looked out my window only to see the earth a mess again. Can you see it with me? The sun, moon and stars were still there, but all of the created creatures were all gone. Also, the birds were all gone, the grass and herbs were gone, but the **sea creatures** were still around though, which was good to know. The earth was unfruitful, therefore it was not a place of beauty for the eye to see. There were no trees or grass as far as the eye could see. The earth looked like a big desert in every direction that I looked, but the sun did shine in the day, therefore the moon gave off her light at night. The earth was not in total chaos in this Third Creation, because the earth had form. Darkness did not overtake it.

Moses was a strange writer because he did not explain the transition that took place between some of the verses. What I mean is that he tells what happen in the last creation, but in chapter 2:4 he tells another story about God's creation that is different from the last creation. All of a sudden, in Genesis 2:4 he begins to tell a story that does not match the last story. But if you know the **secret codes**, it will make sense. Actually, Moses is telling another story contrary to the one he just told us in the last chapter. Moses is telling us that God is renewing the earth again for the third time in this Third Creation of God. The earth had been destroyed by water again, only this time God did not have to create any sea creatures because they were able to survive the flood, because they lived in the water. The earth still had the sun, moon, and stars, so the earth was not frozen over this time between the Second and Third Creations of God.

In this Third Creation, I will show to you that the whole order of God's creation is in a different order from the last creation. I used to think that the creation in the Second Creation, which was in the First Chapter of Genesis, was the same as the creation in this Second Chapter of Genesis, but the Holy Spirit showed to me that these creations where different. I had to keep reading them over and over again until I had a breakthrough, as I was able to hear with my spiritual ears what the Holy Spirit was trying to teach me.

The Bible is no ordinary book, because you cannot read it like other books. It was written by men of God who wrote as they were inspired by the Spirit of God. To be able to understand it, you must read it through your spiritual eyes, not your natural eyes. You must use your spiritual ears, not your natural ears. No one will truly understand it if they only use the intellect of their natural minds. Moses began to tell a story of how God renewed the earth again. The description of the earth is different in this chapter than what it was in the first chapter. Moses said in Genesis 1:2, "The earth was without form, and void; and darkness was on the face of the deep." But now in the second chapter, Moses tells another story of a new beginning. In this third creation of God, things were done much different than in the other creations. By that, I mean the order of God's creation was done in different ways on different days. Watch as I describe how God made the things in this third creation. The second flood that I talked about previously happened between *Genesis 2:3 and 2:4* **(this place is another gap in time, a secret revelation),** because in verse 2:4, Moses talks about the Third Creation of God. He begins by telling about its history. Moses tells how this Third Creation came about. (The gap between these two creations lasted probably eons of years, because of the age of the sun, moon, and stars.) Listen to Moses' story: *Genesis 2:4-7, "(vs. 4) <u>This is the history of the heavens and the earth</u> when they were created, in the day that the Lord* **God made the earth and the heavens, (vs. 5) before any plant of the field was in the earth and before any herb of the field had grown.** *For the Lord God had not caused it to rain on the earth, and <u>there was no man to till the ground</u>; (vs. 6) but a mist went up from the earth and watered the whole face of the ground. (vs. 7) And the* **Lord God formed man of the dust of the ground***, and breathed into his nostrils the breath of life; and man became a living being."*

Moses already told how God made the earth anew in the first chapter of Genesis. Now here in the Second Chapter of Genesis he is going to tell us about how God is going to create everything again. Moses starts in (vs. 4) by saying, **"This is the history of the heavens and the earth when they were created."** Moses is making a statement in the first part of the verse where he is going to tell us a history lessen by explaining how God made the earth new again, in this third creation. He begins by telling us that, **"before**

any herb of the field had grown." God was about to make a man from the dust of the ground. In the last chapter, Moses gave detailed descriptions of how God created everything on the earth before He created the spiritual man in His own image. So now Moses is going to tell what happened after the last creation was destroyed, except for the sea creatures. He tells why things had not grown on the earth in this creation in (vs. 5) "For the Lord God had not caused it to rain on the earth, and there **was no man to till the ground**."

Moses did not say anything like this in the last chapter of Genesis. The reason for this is that God needed a man made of the earth to till the ground in this creation, because God wanted this creation to be different from the last two creations, which were controlled by spirit beings. Moses tells us how God takes some dust of the earth to make this special man. He says that the earth was watered in a special way, in the beginning of this third creation: *"(vs. 6) but a mist went up from the earth and watered the whole face of the ground."*

He gave us two reasons why there is nothing growing on the earth in this Third Creation of God: there was no rain, there was **no man** to till the ground. So this caused me to look a little bit closer at this history lesson. In the last creation, the earth was covered with water. In this creation, the only water was a mist from the ground. In the last creation, Moses said nothing about God needing a man to till the ground. In this creation, God needs a man to till the ground. When I was studying these creations, I was confused because they did not match at all. So I asked the Holy Spirit to give me understanding as to why there were so many differences in the first two chapters of Genesis. In the **second creation,** it only took God six days to do His work of creation. He then rested on the seventh day. Moses did not say anything about the Garden of Eden or the tree of life, nor did God put any tree off limits to the male or female that He created in the Second Creation. God created the spirit male and female after everything else was created. I cannot tell you how many times I had to read these scriptures before I had my breakthrough on their true meaning, through the Holy Spirit's teaching. There are truly many secret key verses in these scriptures that can shed light to help us receive knowledge. Getting back to Moses' story of the third creation of God, he tells us how God created an earthly man from the dust of the earth. "**And the <u>Lord God formed man of the dust of the ground</u>, and breathed into his nostrils the breath of life; and man became a living being**" **(Genesis 2:7).**

In this verse, I saw God taking some dust from the ground to make this man, but in the last Chapter, in Genesis 1:27, God did not make that man from the dust of the ground. God waited a long time for this moment to take place, where He could at last form an earthly man from the dust of the earth. He had everything that He needed to make it happen, therefore He knew that the time was right. In the last creation, which was the Second Creation, God created the spirit male in His own image for this perfect time, to bring together the earthly man and the spirit man into one being. When God formed the man from the dust of the ground, the man had no life in himself at all, until God breathed (Adam's spirit) the breath of life into the man's nostrils (the body without the spirit is dead). The earthly man came to life when that happened.

Just a note on this subject: when I was old enough to know right from wrong, I had a void in my life where I felt kind of empty. I began to seek out something that could fill this emptiness that I had. Nothing I tried seemed to work, until one day a preacher explained to me what I needed. Yes, I asked Jesus into my heart. He caused breath to come into my dead spirit, which gave me new life!

It was an amazing sight to see, as I watched in the Spirit, God making this man from the dust of the ground. But the man that God made from the earth was lifeless in the Master's hand, until an amazing thing happened. **God "breathed into his nostrils the breath of life; and man became a living being." (vs. 7).** When God breathed this breath of life into that man of the dust, he came to life at that very moment. Excitement filled the air as this man came to life. Why, I could almost see God wink His eyes at the man, as he took that first breath of air. God breathed a spirit and soul into the man's body to make him in the like-ness of Himself; three parts, body, soul, spirit. This union of the three parts caused the man to **"became a living being."**

I was amazed to see this happen. It looked like what I saw happen in the last creation, except this time God used earthly material to create the man, instead of spiritual material. I believe God used the spiritual man in the second creation for that purpose, to be placed in the earthly man, in this third creation of God.

In the Third Creation, God formed man from the dust of the ground. There was no life in that man that was formed from the dust of the ground, until God breathed in his nostrils the breath of life, which was the spirit of Adam that came from God. This happened before God created everything else. Much different from the last creation.

Also, there was no mention of how long it took God to create everything in this creation. In this **Third Creation** of God, the sun, moon, and stars were already there. The earth was not flooded over with water either, at the beginning of this creation. The flood waters were gone. God performed an operation on Adam to be able to form a woman from him. Unlike the last creation, God created a spirit man that had a male and female created within himself. They were created at the same time, but in the third creation, the earthly man was created first and then the woman was taken out of him. This was done after Adam named all of the animals. Now I was able to see these first three creations of God, with the Holy Spirit's help. The **First Creation** of God was a testing ground for Lucifer and the other angels who were under his control. The **Second Creation** of God was a testing ground for the spirit man to reign in, which was able to fill the earth. The **Third Creation** of God was the testing ground for the earthly man to reign over the earth. You see, God said in His word that He knew us before we were born. *Jeremiah 1:5,* "**Before I formed you in the womb I knew you;** **Before you were born** *I sanctified you; I ordained you a prophet to the nations."* I believe that Jeremiah's spirit was created in the Second Creation of God as well as Adam's spirit.

111

Because God said that He knew Jeremiah before his flesh was born, Jeremiah's spirit is the real person, not his flesh, because the flesh is just the housing or tent of the spiritual man.

The spiritual realm, during the Second Creation of God, is where God created the first spiritual male and female. He placed them on the earth to multiply and fill the earth. He gave them authority to have dominion over all the creation. At that time, I am sure that Satan was displeased at that decision made by God, to put the spiritual man in charge of the earth, because he used to be in charge of it until his fall. But the fact remains, God gave the spirit man the right to rule the earth. By you and me being able to go back in time on this journey, we were able to see how or why God had different stages of His creation.

We will never know all of the facts of God's creation until we get to the other side of glory, where we will be with Jesus, for we will see Him face-to-face in all of His glory. There is a huge difference between the two creations if you look at them closely, as we have studied so far. Come with me on this voyage as I look at the differences in the next few verses.

LIFE IN THE GARDEN FROM MY TIME CAPSULE

Adam was created "**before any plant of the field was in the earth and before any herb of the field had grown**" (*Genesis 2:5*). In this Second Chapter of Genesis, God formed man from the dust of the ground (vs. 7), before any plant or herb, also before any living creatures that breathe air like humans. In (vs. 7), God made Adam from the dust of the earth, and man became a living being. In (vs. 8), "*The Lord God* **planted a garden eastward in Eden**, *and there He put the man whom He formed.*" This is the first garden that God planted in this chapter. This garden was planted for the man to live in, until God was done making the main Garden of Eden. After I watched God forming the man of the dust, I looked on as the Lord God planted a garden east of Eden.

This garden was not the Garden of Eden. It was a garden that stretched around the world. I say that because the rest of the trees and grass had to be created in that duration, as you can see in (vs. 9), "*And* **out of the ground the Lord God made every tree grow** *that is pleasant to the sight and good for food. The tree of life was also in the midst of the garden, and the tree of the knowledge of good and evil.*" In (vs. 9) is the **secret of wisdom and understanding**. If

God created the trees in Chapter 1, why did He have to create them again in chapter 2? We have already seen why there are two different creations in these two chapters. The trees were destroyed in the second creation in Chapter 1. Now we see God bringing forth out of the ground trees once again. In the first garden, God made from the ground the trees and herbs for the rest of the world, which was considered to be eastward of Eden. Now in (vs. 9), God makes the Garden of Eden from the ground with special trees that are of significant value: **The tree of life** *was also in the midst of the garden, and* **the tree of the knowledge of good and evil.** The tree of life was none other than Jesus Christ. **The tree of the knowledge of good and evil** was the forbidden tree that they were not to eat from. I will talk about it later on.

As I looked from my window of the time capsule, I could see the two gardens were beautiful for the eyes to behold. I was allowed to step down from my time capsule to go outside for one moment, so that I could get some fresh air. The moment I took some fresh air into my nostrils, it was as if I had new life coming into my body. There was no smoke or pollution in this air, for it was pure air, filtered God's way. At that moment I realized this was the reason people could live much longer than us. Also there were no viruses or sickness or diseases in that duration of time. I could see the great rivers flowing through the Garden of Eden very clearly; **"from there it parted and became four riverheads"** *(vs. 10).* I felt as though I was in heaven itself. Just take some time right now to meditate on God's word on this subject. Close your eyes to see this Garden of Eden through your inner man, by the Holy Spirit. Can you see the beauty of the perfect trees with their good fruit on them? Can you see the river flowing? What is missing from the sounds that you hear? There are no animals or birds or chipmunks running through the Garden.

Everything was silent except for the breeze that was blowing. I could hear the sound of the water from the river that was flowing. In the Second Creation, I talked about how everything was created before man, but in this Third Creation, man was created before all of the rest of God's creation. This is why you could not hear any of those creatures running around in the garden. Can you see why I believe in three creations? There are not a lot of scriptures on this subject, but there are **hidden secrets** in them, if you dig deeper into them. When God finished the Garden of Eden, He took the man He had formed from the dust of the ground: **Genesis 2:15, "Then the Lord God took the man and put him in the Garden of Eden to tend**

and keep it." Here God took the man out of the first garden to place him in the Garden of Eden to be its caretaker. As of yet, the man (Adam) did not have any woman with him, which was strange, because in the first chapter of Genesis, the male and female were together all of the time. There was no mention of the Garden of Eden in the first chapter either, nor was the tree of life mentioned or the tree of knowledge of good and evil.

Look at (vs. 9): "*And* **out of the ground the Lord God made every tree grow**.*"* God made every tree grow out of the earth. In this Third Creation, God made things grow from the ground rather than creating it out of nothing. Man (Adam) was made from the earth first, then all other things were made from the ground after him. In the First Creation, God created the heavens and the earth out of nothing. In the Second Creation, God created some things from nothing except the trees, grass, and so forth, because He said, "Let the earth bring them forth." Also the living creatures. He said, "Let the earth bring forth." God wanted certain things to be made of earthly material. In both the Second Creation and the Third Creation, God made those things from the earth. As I was admiring the beautiful Garden of Eden, I saw God take the man He had created and placed him in the Garden of Eden.

When God placed him in this garden, He gave the man His first command. *Genesis 2:16, 17, "And the Lord God commanded the man, saying, 'Of every tree of the garden you may freely eat; (vs. 17.) But of* the **tree of the knowledge of good and evil you shall not eat**, *for in the day that you eat of it you shall surely die.'"* In the last creation there were no trees off limits because the tree of life or the tree of the knowledge of good and evil were not placed on the earth at that time.

Nor was there a Garden of Eden in the Second Creation of God. It was only mentioned in the Third Creation. Even the serpent was not mentioned in the Second Creation. Now in this Third Creation, the Garden of Eden was ready for the man of the earth to take care of it. This is the reason the Lord God took the man out of the other garden to place him in the Garden of Eden. In the first instructions to the man from the Lord God, there is one tree that is off limits to Adam: *"the* **tree of the knowledge of good and evil you shall not eat**.*"* God told him he would die if he ate of that tree. Here again we can find wisdom from God our creator,

God created this man, made from the dust of the earth, to live forever. If he had obeyed God's command, he would have lived forever, both in body and spirit. But if he ate of the forbidden tree, God said,

"*You shall surely die.*" The implication of that action would bring two kinds of death to the man of the earth. I will explain more about it as we go forward on our journey.

A HELPMATE FOR ADAM

This Third Creation was so much different from the last creation. Take for instance these next few verses. Pay close attention to the way God made things in those verses. Since you have been with me on this journey, you were able to see first-hand how God created everything in all of those creations on this earth. I have found that if I read the scriptures carefully within my spiritual man, by listening to the Holy Spirit I found out there are deeper meanings within the scriptures than I was used to. Watch with me as I witnessed one of the greatest miracles about to happen. You will notice with me how God pulled something out of the earth after Adam had been formed.

Genesis 2:18, "And the Lord God said, 'it is not good that man should be alone; I will make him a helper comparable to him.'" God was talking to His Son and the Holy Spirit, for they all worked as one, but Adam heard Him speak those things as well. Adam wondered what his helpmate was going to look like. I am sure of that, as we will observe later on. It looked as though he was on the edge of his seat as God began to do His creating. *Genesis 2:19, "__Out of the ground__ the _Lord God formed every beast_ of the field and every bird of the air, and brought them to Adam to see what he would call them. And whatever Adam called each living creature that was its name."* Here God forms all of the creatures again, only this time He forms them after Adam was formed. Out of the earth, God began to form all of the creatures of the field as well as the birds of the air. Again, I believe that God reached into the earth to pull the bones of the different animals out of it, then formed each one into its original shape. It was so amazing to watch God at work. All of the creatures were made at lightning speed.

The interesting thing I observed was that there was no mention of the sea creatures in this Third Creation of God. That was because they were not destroyed from the last creation (the second creation). Everything started to look like the things I used to see in my old creation before I left on this journey in my time capsule. I saw every kind of creature on the earth, moving about on the ground, as well as the birds of the air. The Garden of Eden became a place of many sounds as the creatures made their presence known. Adam was amazed at all of the creatures that God formed from the earth. As he was admiring them, God, **"brought them to Adam to see what he would call them. And whatever Adam called each living creature, that was its name" (vs. 2:19).**

It looked like Adam was enjoying his task of naming all of the creatures, but he did not find any of them to be his helpmate. In the last creation, the man and female were not given the job of naming these creatures, but in this creation Adam was given that job. This is another reason to believe that there is more than one creation. You will discover more in the verses that follow. *Genesis 2:20, "So Adam gave names to all cattle, to the birds of the air, and to every beast of the field. But <u>for Adam there was not found a helper comparable to him."</u>* After Adam got done naming all of those creatures, he did not see one of them that was comparable to himself. I could see that he was bummed out, as I would say in my day, but God had a plan to make Adam one like himself.

CAN A MAN HAVE A WOMAN IN HIMSELF?

What I saw next would shock anyone who might observe this act that God performed. **Genesis 2:21, "And the Lord God caused a deep sleep to fall on Adam, and he slept; and He took one of his**

ribs, and closed up the flesh in its place." God performed an operation on Adam because God saw a helpmate inside of Adam that was comparable to him. To get this helpmate out of Adam, God had to perform an operation. I saw God put Adam in a deep sleep, deep enough so that Adam could not feel God's knife penetrate through his skin. But the interesting thing I saw was that God removed one of Adam's ribs. All I saw was the rib, but God saw a helpmate for Adam, instead of a rib. God saw the finished product before it took its final shape. God saw a woman before He took Adam's rib in His hands. God then proceeded to close up the wound in Adam's side. This sure was different from the second creation we just visited, because in the last creation, the male and the female were created at the same time, but in this creation Adam was created much earlier than the woman. Not only that, but in this creation the woman was taken out of Adam, days later after Adam was created. It took Adam a long time to name all of the animals.

I was not told how long it took Adam to name the animals, it seemed to be a long time. Now comes the fun part of our trip on this journey through time. God held Adam's rib firmly in His hand as He begin to form a woman out of that rib. What a sight to behold. I was stunned by this great transformation. She was very beautiful, as all of God's creations are. Then God presented the woman alive to Adam. **Genesis 2:22, "Then the rib which the Lord God had taken from man He made into a woman, and He brought her to the man."**

Finally Adam saw his helpmate. What a sight to behold indeed, as I saw Adam's face light up with a smile of great joy. Even though there were no clothes on her, Adam had no lustful thoughts because he did not know right from wrong.

Genesis 2:23, "And Adam said: 'This is now bone of my bones and flesh of my flesh; she shall be called Woman, because she was taken out of man.'"

Adam even got to name her because she was also part of the creation of God. Adam knew that she was made from his rib because he mentioned it in the last scripture above. Adam was delighted to have Eve as his helpmate because they were of the same flesh. When Adam looked at Eve, he saw himself because the two of them became one flesh. **Genesis 2:24, 25, "Therefore a man shall leave his father and mother and be joined to his wife, and they shall become one flesh. (25.) And they both were naked, the man and his wife, and they were not ashamed."**

Thought #1: For this reason' (vs. 24) **a man will leave his father and mother to be united to his wife, they will become one flesh.** Please take note of the things in these scriptures:

(1.) God put the man into a deep sleep to perform an operation on the man, by taking one of his ribs out. (2.) God made a woman from that rib He had taken out of the man. Notice: God made a woman from that rib. He did not create her, but made her from the rib. He did not form her, but made her out of the rib. It is here that God pulled out of Adam one of his ribs to form the woman, at which time I believe God pulled the female spirit out of Adam's spirit, to cause the fleshly woman to receive life. Then God presented her alive to Adam. This is proof that God has within Himself everything He needs to be the God you can approach to be fed. He is the same God who can heal your broken body.

Let me give you another thought: Does the Holy Spirit come to man or woman in different forms? Why, of course not! We are **all one with Him**, both male and female. We become one with Him, by the new birth in the Spirit by the Holy Spirit of God.

Thought #2: If our spirit did not originate from Adam's spirit, the spiritual part of us would not have been born in sin, for it would not have been in the Garden of Eden with Adam. Spirit produces spirit, and flesh produces flesh. That which is flesh is flesh and that which is spirit is spirit, for the flesh was not first, but the spirit, then was the flesh. In every man or every woman there is the ability to produce a child, which could be either a boy or girl. That means one thing: in every man and woman, there are living embryos that are x or y, meaning male and female. This can happen when a man and woman come together in a relationship with each other. At this time, a union of the male sperm and the female eggs can produce a child in the womb of the woman.

We know that God was talking to the spirit male and female that He created in verse 1:27. He told them to be fruitful and to increase in number and to fill the earth and subdue it. In Genesis 2:7 comes the union of the earthly man and the spirit man, in which the earthly man receives life: (vs. 7)*"the Lord God formed the man from the dust of the ground and breathed into his nostrils the breath of life, and the man became a living being."* It is here that God made the earthly man, so that he could place the spirit of Adam in the man of the earth, which was Adam's flesh, which caused the earthly man to live.

When God made the man of the earth, He did not tell him to be fruitful and multiply at the time of His creation. I found that interesting, until I read in the scriptures that God has nothing to do with the flesh. For in the flesh dwells no good thing. God is Spirit and talks to the spirit of man. In the Garden He spoke to the spirit of Adam, the real person, but when Adam sinned he died spiritually, losing fellowship with God. It is after Adam and Eve sinned that God gave them their sentence of death, for He had told them in **Genesis 2:17, "but you must not eat from the tree of the knowledge of good and evil, for when you eat of it you will surely die."**

Thought #3. For He said in the Garden of Eden: **(Genesis 3:22, 23) "And the Lord God said, 'The man has now become like one of us, knowing good and evil. <u>He must not be allowed to reach out his hand and take also from the tree of life and eat, and live forever.</u>' So the Lord God banished him from the Garden of Eden to work the ground from which he had been taken."** God formed all things in (Gen. 2:9); also in (vs. 2:19), from the earth itself after Adam was created. The earth itself was created by God out of nothing, in the very first creation that we talked about earlier in this book.

But now we see that God forms the rest of the things out of the earth in the Second Chapter of Genesis. The sea creatures were not mentioned here because they were able to exist and live in water and therefore were not affected by the floods. With the spoken word from God's lips in Genesis 1:11-13, the earth brought forth all of the things listed therein. It did not say that God formed them but commanded the earth to bring them forth. In the next Chapter, Adam and Eve, were about to get an uninvited guest in the Garden of Eden, which would change the history of humanity.

Chapter Seven

LUCIFER, HOW ARE YOU FALLEN FROM HEAVEN!

Isaiah 14:12, 13, (vs. 12) *"How you are fallen from heaven, O Lucifer, son of the morning! How you are cut down to the ground, You who weakened the nations! (vs. 13) For you have said in your heart: I will ascend into heaven, I will exalt my throne above the stars of God; I will also sit on the mount of the congregation On the farthest sides of the north;"* Genesis 3:1, *"Now the serpent was more cunning than any beast of the field which the Lord God had made."* I saw in the spirit a serpent appeared out of nowhere. The serpent, Lucifer (Satan) was in disguise so that he could fool Eve. You see, Satan was angry that he lost his power over the earth when he sinned against God, so he needed a way to get his power back. I am not sure what influence Lucifer had in the Second Creation,

but I know that in this Third Creation, in which we now live, he has a lot of power and influence in the world.

"The serpent was more cunning than any beast of the field" (vs. 1). This serpent was no ordinary snake because he was craftier, plus he was more deceptive than any other beast of the field. That was because the serpent was possessed by Satan himself. With that being said, I could see that the serpent was an interesting snake, who was very crafty in all of his ways. Eve had no idea that it was Satan, who was using the serpent to deceive her into sinning against God. Plus, Eve had no knowledge of right or wrong. Lucifer (the serpent) now had a chance to regain his power over the earth that he lost when he sinned against God in the First Creation. Isaiah 14:12, 3, *"How you are fallen from heaven, O Lucifer, son of the morning!"* (Lucifer was mentioned in the first creation, where he was the ruler of the earth during that duration of time. In the Second Creation he became known as Darkness, who had lost his power. Other than that, he was not talked about in that Second Creation of God at all. In this Third Creation he appeared as a serpent (Satan). He regained his power because of the fall of man.)

Genesis 3:1, **"Now the serpent was more cunning than any beast of the field which the Lord God had made. And he said to the woman, 'Has**

God indeed said, "You shall not eat of every tree of the garden"?'"

The serpent knew that if he could trick the woman into eating of the forbidden fruit, he would gain victory over the human race that God created. The conversation between the serpent and the woman was about to change the course of the earth by one act of disobedience by the woman and the man. As I watched from my time capsule, things seemed to be getting much heated up. The serpent began to throw one question after another at the woman to try to confuse her in her thinking about what God told her in the first place. This was for sure no ordinary serpent, because he had a way of changing words around, so that he could confuse the woman. By the way, I never heard of a snake talking to anybody, have you? Except this time, the serpent knew what God had said, but was convinced that he could trick the woman. He knew very well what God had said. He knew there was only one tree off limits to them. I saw the serpent lick his chops as he waited for the woman to respond to his questions.

(Vs. 2, 3), "And the woman said to the serpent, 'We may eat the fruit of the trees of the garden; but of the fruit of the tree which is in the midst of

the garden, God has said, "You shall not eat it, nor shall you touch it, lest you die.""

Lucifer did not want the woman or the man to rule the earth, so he went to work out a plan that would cause them to lose their ownership of that right to rule the earth. So now, the serpent attacked the woman's mind with words that caused her to sin against God.

Genesis 3:4, 5, (vs. 4) "Then the serpent said to the woman, 'You will not surely die. (Vs. 5) For God knows that in the day you eat of it your eyes will be opened, and you will be like God, knowing good and evil.'" The serpent painted a picture in her mind. By saying that she would not die, he also said that she would become like God, knowing good and evil. By looking at these verses, can you see how the devil could trick us into sinning against God? *Surely, God will not kill you! You will become like Him, if you eat that fruit you will know good and evil, you will be like God Himself.*

Pay close attention to what kind of thoughts enter your mind when you are being tempted to sin against God, because that same serpent that tempted Eve will also tempt you and me. The woman was pure, free from sin before the serpent came to her because she did not know right from wrong. She only knew that she was not to touch one tree that was in the middle of the garden. The serpent knew that she had no knowledge of good or evil, so he began to play mind games with her on the subject of the tree. He spoke the words, (vs. 4) **"You will not surely die."** He did not stop there, he told her something else: (vs. 5) **"For God knows that in the day you eat of it your eyes will be opened, and you will be like God, knowing good and evil."** "Yes, you will be like God," is the thought he imparted into her mind. He gave her a thought that would give her power to be like God. All of creation was affected by that decision she made on that day. All of humanity, plus every creature of the earth, was affected by that decision of the woman and the man. Now that the serpent had placed those thoughts into the mind of the woman, she now began to look at the tree in a different way.

Genesis 3:6, "So when the woman saw that the tree was good for food, that it was pleasant to the eyes, and a tree desirable to make one wise, she took of its fruit and ate. She also gave to her husband with her, and he ate."

Now all of a sudden, the tree that was forbidden to the woman became pleasant to her eyes. Although the tree was the same tree as before, it appeared different to the woman at this time. The reason it looked different to her this time was because the serpent used enticing words to the woman's ears, which changed her thoughts on how the tree looked. The tree was not only looking good to her, but it also became more appealing to her because it could make her wise. The action that the woman was about to do would change the whole history of humanity forever. **"She took of its fruit and ate. She also gave to her husband with her, and he ate." (vs. 6).** It did not become sin until she took of its fruit. She not only ate the fruit, but she gave some to her husband to eat. Eve was deceived into sinning against God by eating the fruit of the tree, but Adam was not deceived, because he ate freely ate it by his own will. Therefore, he was guilty of the crime. From my time capsule, I watched the event unfold right before my eyes in the spirit. I screamed out at them, "Do not touch the fruit, "but they could not see me or hear me because I was invisible to them. Chills ran through my body as they took their first bite, because I knew what the outcome of their disobedience would bring forth. One thing I noticed here: the serpent did not encourage Eve to partake of a better tree, which was the Tree of Life. It was there within her reach. It was not off limits to her until she ate of the wrong tree first.

She could have had eternal life if she would have eaten it first, in which case she would have lived forever if she took of its fruit. This was why the serpent had her focus on the forbidden tree so that it would bring death to her. By her doing that, the serpent was given power over the earth once again. All of God's creation stood still for a moment until that action was taken. After they both had partaken of the fruit, everything began to change in a moment of time. Yes, the serpent was leaping for joy because he knew that the earth would belong to him. He would once again be the ruler of the earth, for a long time.

For the life of me, I could not figure out why God, the Creator of all things, would let those things take place. If God knows all things ahead of time, why did He not stop that serpent from deceiving the woman into taking of the fruit? God knows everything. He has a plan already worked out before anything happens. He created man to have a free will, to choose right from wrong. He did not want to create a robot. He created man to become like Him. He created us to be beings of choice, to know right from wrong. God created the man and the woman with a free will that would give them a choice, to make a decision, to eat fruit from a tree or not to eat of its fruit. He created all of us with a free will to make choices to do right or wrong things. But the choice that Adam and Eve made that day affected all of God's creations. All of us have to make choices in our lives, from the very day we sinned.

God gives us a free will to do what we want, so we can choose life or death, to choose to be a slave to sin or to be free from sin, as long as we choose to be one of God's children. The choice that Adam and Eve made that day brought them into a new realm of discovery they had never been in before, a realm of the unknown, a realm of seeing things in a different light. Why, they had a new knowledge of knowing right from wrong, which they did not have before eating of the forbidden fruit. All of a sudden, they were ashamed of being naked because of this new knowledge of good and evil.

That is why we find them looking for something to make clothes out of. Look at the next verse in **Genesis 3:7, "Then the eyes of both of them were opened, and they knew that they were naked; and they sewed fig leaves together and made themselves coverings."** Their eyes were opened: what does that mean? Were they created with no sight? Of course not, they were created with perfect sight. Something happened to their eyes when they partook of the forbidden fruit. A new avenue of their sight was coming into view. The knowledge of good and evil came into contact with their spiritual eyes, causing them to see things with a new understanding. All of a sudden, they knew that they were naked, so they made themselves a covering for their bodies, to hide their shame. As I looked from my time capsule, it was like looking at a movie on the big screen TV, in my former life. Everything in God's creation changed in a moment of time. The creatures who used to get along were now enemies to each other. I looked to my right as I heard the sound of God the Creator, speaking from the other side of the Garden.

"Adam. Adam where are you?"

I knew then that Adam was going to be in big trouble.

Genesis 3:7,8, "And they heard the sound of the Lord God walking in the garden in the cool of the day, and Adam and his wife hid themselves from the presence of the Lord God among the trees of the garden. Then the Lord God called to Adam and said to him, 'Where are you?'"

No one can hide from the Lord God, so why did He ask Adam where he was? God knew where Adam was in the natural realm, but He knew that Adam was not in the place of fellowship where He last had contact with him. Adam was spiritually dead to God because he had sinned against the Lord God, by partaking of the forbidden fruit. That was why God said to Adam, "Where are you? I do not feel connected to you anymore." God knew where Adam was in the natural, therefore God knew something was wrong with Adam's spiritual condition. God, who is perfect in every way, did not know what sin felt like, for He never sinned, therefore God never experienced sin's effect in His own body. Even though God could not feel the pain of sin, He did have a plan already in place to fix the problem that Adam was facing. "Adam, where are you? I do not know you in the condition you are in. Your spirit seems to be dead to Me."

Genesis 3:10, 11, "So he said, 'I heard Your voice in the garden, and I was afraid because I was naked; and I hid myself.' And He said, 'Who told you that you were naked? Have you eaten from the tree of which I commanded you that you should not eat?'"

I could see that this was a very difficult time for Adam because he now had to give an account for that action that he took in eating of the forbidden fruit. I could see him looking over at his wife, as he looked for words to say.

Genesis 3:12, "Then the man said, 'The woman whom You gave to be with me, she gave me of the tree, and I ate.'" Adam tried to put the blame on his wife, thinking that would free him from the wrongdoing.

It is from this place in history that we have inherited our bad nature or our sinful ways. "*For all have sinned and came short of the glory of God*" *(Romans 3:23)*. "You gave me this woman who gave me the fruit, so I ate." I think that we all do the same thing as Adam. We like to blame someone else for our wrongdoing. Judgment was about to fall on the earth because of their act of disobedience. Come with me as I go on this journey a little further.

Chapter Eight

THE CURSES FROM ADAM'S SIN

Genesis 3:13, 14, (vs. 13) "And the Lord God said to the woman, 'What is this you have done?' The woman said, 'The serpent deceived me, and I ate.' (vs. 14) So the Lord God said to the serpent: 'Because you have done this, <u>You are cursed </u>more than all cattle, And more than every beast of the field; On your belly you shall go, And you shall eat dust All the days of your life.'"

Just one act of disobedience caused all of God's created beings to be cursed. God is a righteous judge who will give everybody a chance to defend their unrighteous acts before He passes judgment on them.

First, God asked Adam a very simple question, *"Where are you*?" God did not say anything to Adam about his disobedience to Him, He simply asked where he was. Adam, at this time, knew right from wrong so he knew that he needed to explain where he was. On the other hand, God knew that Adam was not in the same place where He left him. God felt a disconnection between their spirits. Because Adam received this new knowledge from the forbidden fruit, it caused him to become fearful for the first time in his life, **(vs. 10) "So he said, 'I heard Your voice in the garden, and I was afraid because I was naked; and I hid myself.'"**

"The fear of God is the beginning of wisdom" (Proverbs 1:7). Adam knew that he had sinned, therefore he tried to hide from God's presence. At that time, Adam's ears could hear God's voice calling out his name. Now in God's righteous judgment, He asked Adam another question in His investigation into the act of Adam's sin. **(vs. 11) "And He said, 'Who told you that you were naked? Have you eaten from the tree of which I commanded you that you should not eat?'"** In other words, God was telling Adam that he would not have known that he was naked unless someone told him, therefore if no one told him, the only way of knowing that he was naked was that he must have eaten of the forbidden fruit. Then Adam confessed to God that it was "The woman that You gave to me, she is the one who gave the fruit to me, so I ate it." God had enough information from Adam, so he questioned the woman next. **(vs. 13) "And the Lord God said to the woman, 'What is this you have done?' The woman said, 'The serpent deceived me, and I ate.'"**

It is from Adam and Eve that we inherit the thing we call "the blame game." I believe that every one of us has played this game in our journey here on this earth. I am guilty of it many times in my life time, until I was taught by Pastor David L. Thomas not to blame others. I was taught to take responsibility for my own actions.

THE FIRST CURSE FROM GOD

"So the Lord God said to the serpent: 'Because you have done this, <u>You are cursed </u>more than all cattle, And more than every beast of the field; On your belly you shall go, And you shall eat dust All the days of your life'" (vs. 14).

The serpent received the first curse from God because he had done the act of deceiving the woman into sinning, therefore he was reduced to a creature that had to craw on its belly. He was cursed more than all cattle and beasts of the field. Then God also said something else to the serpent: **(vs. 15) "And I will put enmity Between you and the woman, And between your seed and her Seed; He shall bruise** your head, And you shall bruise His heel." We are not going to study all of the meaning of these verses in this book. We are here to study about the creation in general.

Now we will look at the curse of the woman. God told the serpent (Satan) that He was going to put enmity between their seeds. Now watch for the key word of who this enmity is in the second part of the verse: "**He shall bruise your head.**" Who is the only one who can bruise the head of the serpent (Satan)? Why, of course, it is Jesus Christ. Then God told the serpent: "**And you shall bruise His heel.**" The serpent did that in the New Testament, when Jesus went to the cross. But when Jesus was raised from the grave that was when Christ bruised Satan's head. "Her **Seed**" refers to Jesus Christ, who came through her (Adam and Eve's) lineage. Satan is the enemy of our soul for sure. Lucifer (Satan) was already cursed because of his rebellion against God, but now the serpent who was possessed by Satan, received a curse also, along with everything on the earth.

THE SECOND CURSE: THE CURSE OF THE WOMAN.

Genesis 3:16, "To the woman He said, 'I will greatly multiply your sorrow and your conception;

In pain you shall bring forth children; Your desire shall be for your husband, And he shall rule over you.'" Because of her sin, she was to have much sorrow, therefore in childbirth she would have pain. This meant that if she had not sinned, she might not have had any pain with childbirth. But because of the curse of sin, pain and sorrow would be a part of her life.

THE THIRD CURSE: THE CURSE OF ADAM

Now it was time for God to give Adam his punishment for his sin by placing a curse on him. Adam's curse was twofold. First, God cursed the ground for his sake. Second, God cursed him to death, meaning Adam now was going to die physically in the near future. He not only died spiritually when he sinned, he now was going to die physically also.

Genesis 3:17-19, "Then to Adam He said, 'Because you have heeded the voice of your wife, and have eaten from the tree of which I commanded you, saying, "You shall not eat of it"; Cursed is the ground for your sake; In toil you shall eat of it All the days of your life. Both thorns and thistles it shall bring forth for you, And you shall eat the herb of the field. In the sweat of your face you shall eat bread <u>Till you return to the ground, For</u>

out of it you were taken; For dust you are, And to dust you shall return.'"

The promise of death to Adam's physical body was pronounced in the last part of this verse, "**And to dust you shall return,**" when God told him that he would die, if he ate of the forbidden fruit. Adam's right to live forever was turned into a sentence of death.

This was a long journey for us to take, but I hope you learned something along the way. It is time for us to head back toward our old place were we used to be. We have at least one more stop along the way, somewhere in Rome.

CREATION EAGERLY WAITS FOR REDEMPTION

Romans 8:18-23, "(vs. 18) For I considered that the suffering of this present time are not worthy to be compared with the glory which shall be revealed in us. (vs. 19) For the earnest expectation of the creation eagerly waits for the revealing of the sons of God. (vs. 20) For the creation was subjected to futility, not willingly, but because of Him who subjected it in hope; (vs. 21) because the creation itself also will be delivered from the bondage of corruption into the glorious liberty of the

children of God. (vs. 22) For we know that the whole creation groans and labors with birth pains together until now. (vs. 23) Not only that, but we also who have the first fruits of the Spirit, even we ourselves groan within ourselves, eagerly waiting for the adoption, the redemption of our body."

All of God's creation suffered from the sin of Adam and *"eagerly waits for the revealing of the sons of God."* Because of Adam's sin, all of creation was put under a curse, even though none of them sinned. I have come to a place on our journey in our time capsule somewhere in Rome, where Paul had something to say unto us in the scriptures we just read. All of God's creation: *(vs. 19) "eagerly waits for the revealing of the sons of God."* All of God's creation was in bondage from the moment it was cursed in the beginning of this creation. *"(vs. 22) For we know that the whole creation groans and labors with birth pains together until now."* The whole earth is in birth pains but is waiting for its total redemption from the bondage it is under. *"(vs. 23) Not only that, but we also who have the first fruits of the Spirit, even we ourselves groan within ourselves, eagerly waiting for the adoption, the redemption of our body."* The time for our total redemption and the redemption of all of creation is fast approaching. We are looking forward to the day that our bodies will be redeemed from being corrupt, to bodies that will last forever. All of God's creation will be redeemed from being in the bondage of sin. Our next stop on this journey will take us to the third flood that will destroy the earth with water. Everything will not be destroyed this time, nor will God have to renew the earth again in this third creation of God.

Chapter Nine

THE LAST FLOOD #3

Genesis 9:12-17, "(vs. 12) And God said: 'This is the sign of the covenant which I make between Me and you, and every living creature that is with you, for perpetual generations: (vs. 13) **I set My rainbow in the cloud, and it shall be for the sign of the covenant between Me and the earth.** *(vs. 14) It shall be, when I bring a cloud over the earth, that <u>the rainbow</u> shall be seen in the cloud; (vs. 15) and I will remember My covenant which is between Me and you and every living creature of all flesh;* <u>**the waters shall never again become a flood to destroy all flesh.**</u> *(vs. 16) The <u>rainbow</u> shall be in the cloud, and I will look on it to remember the everlasting covenant between God and every living creature of all flesh that is on the earth.' (vs. 17)*

And God said to Noah, 'This is the sign of the covenant which I have established between Me and all flesh on the earth.'"

No one will ever know all the mysteries of heaven or all the mysteries of the earth. In these last days, God will reveal some of them to His children as we get closer to His return. According to the scriptures I just read, this is the last flood that will ever flood the whole earth. This final flood that God brought on the earth was different from all the others that I talked about previously in this book.

First: In this flood, God had mercy on Noah and his family by saving them from the floodwaters. He also saved a male and female of every kind of living thing on the earth from the floodwaters, by allowing them to enter the Ark with Noah and his family. The trees, along with all other vegetation, were spared, also the sea creatures were spared because they live in water anyway.

{Let me remind you about the order of the three floods that I talked about so far in this book. The **first flood** was in Genesis 1:2. The **second flood** was between Genesis 2:3-4. Then the **third and final flood** was in Genesis 7:17-24.}

Genesis 6:3, "And the Lord said, 'My Spirit shall not strive with man forever, for he is indeed flesh; yet <u>his days shall be one hundred and twenty years</u>.'"

Second: God did not have to re-create the earth again after this third flood, like the other floods. Noah, his family, and all the creatures that were in the Ark were safe from the floodwaters. God did not have to make any more animals or creatures of the earth after this particular flood. God's word is so real, all you need to do is to only believe what it says is true. I found a secret meaning to "Ask," "Seek," "Knock." It did happen when I got desperate. I found all of this knowledge about God's creations. I laid my life down at the mercy of the Holy Spirit, to teach me all about the creations of God, so that I might understand why and how they were created.

"In the beginning God created the heavens and the earth" (Genesis 1:1).

May I try to give you a paraphrase to explain their existence? In the beginning of the heavens and the earth's creation, it was God who created them. In the atmosphere that they were created in, they were created perfect for what purpose God created them for. The phrase, *"In the beginning,"* could not refer to God's beginning, because He is eternal, with no beginning or ending. It refers to the first earth and the heaven's beginning. Although we are not told how long they were created in that state, I am sure that it was many years ago. Some time in that duration of time, God put Lucifer in charge of it because the Bible tells us that he (Lucifer) had a kingdom. One day, who knows how long ago it was, Lucifer rebelled against God, causing God to flood the earth, as I was able to see in the next verse: **Genesis 1:2, "The earth was without form, and void; and darkness was on the face of the deep."** This is the place where we can find the second creation of God.

In the Second Creation; can you see it with me? There is something strange about what it looked like, the earth was full of darkness. Lucifer was cast down as its ruler because of his rebellion. He was the brightest of all of the angels, but now he became darkness, stripped of his power, therefore the earth was without light, full of darkness and covered with water, in total chaos. But God came back to the earth to give it a makeover. God predetermined when He created the earth, that He made it to last forever. God sent His Spirit to move over the waters, which were probably frozen because there was no heat source of any kind, until the Spirit of God begin to move over it. *"Then God said, 'Let there be light,' and there was light."* Jesus, who was the Son of God, showed up, who was Light. The waters melted back to pure water because of the light and heat. Then God did His marvelous work of creation. In the second creation, God decided to put someone else in charge of His creation, now that He put it back into a perfect creation after six days. On the 6 day, God created a spirit man in His own image. He then put him in charge over all of the created things, giving him dominion over them. He gave them (the male and female that were in the spiritual man) power to multiply and fill the earth. (Genesis 1:28) Here in this second creation is a creation consisting of spiritual males and females that were to be in charge of the earth. But these sons of God were made in God's likeness. They were perfect beings, whose purpose was to fill the earth. This creation of God could have lasted many years also, which makes sense, because God created the sun, moon, and stars in that creation. So if we could find out the age of the sun, we would know how long that creation lasted.

By the time the Third Creation of God was discovered, it too was a barren land. It had no trees, herbs, or grass, but it had the sun, moon, and stars in place already. The fish and sea creatures were present also. So the Second Creation was flooded over but receded back to its original place, when God came back to give the earth a makeover again. The Third Creation of God is the one we now live in. It will end as we know it, some time in the future. I hope this review will help you as we go further on our journey.

Chapter Ten

EZEKIEL'S VISION OF REVELATION 19

The next stop on our journey will be in the days of Ezekiel, who was a prophet of God in the Old Testament. I took you to the first three creations of God already in the previous ten chapters. To get us to the next creation of God, it required me to do a lot of research in the Bible. There are many secrets in the Bible that will lead us to the Fourth Creation of God. This Fourth Creation was very hard for me to find, mainly because I was never taught anything about it. Again, I needed the Holy Spirit to help me find this fourth creation. He enlightened me about some key secrets that were hidden in the Bible.

The Holy Spirit prompted me to study the book of Ezekiel first, starting with the 37th chapter, after I read Revelation Chapters 19-22. I had to clear my mind of any old teaching on the subject of the end times, so that I could clearly hear what the Holy Spirit was trying to teach me on this subject. The people had a deaf ear many times to Ezekiel's prophecies, for they just did not want to listen to him. After hearing that, I did not want to be like them. I began to seek answers from God so that I could learn what was really going to happen in the latter days. Please come with me as I take this journey into the unknown world of the fourth creation of God. My first stop will be in Ezekiel 37.

THE DRY BONES LIVE

If we are going to see what is going to happen in Revelation 19, we must look in the book of Ezekiel to get his view on the subject. So for now we will have to take a trip back in time to when Ezekiel was alive. We are going back to the years 500-565 BC. I hope I can find the answers that each of us are looking for, as I go back in time one more time. Come with me to see that Ezekiel had a similar experience to John, who wrote in Revelation 19. Ezekiel was caught up in the Spirit of the Lord: *Ezekiel 37:1, "The hand of the Lord came on me and brought me out in the Spirit of the Lord, and set me down in the midst of the valley; and it was full of bones."* The Lord works in many ways, for this must have seemed strange for Ezekiel to see a valley full of dry bones. Everywhere he looked there were dry bones. He found himself in the middle of them in this valley. I am sure that Ezekiel was not pleased to be there in that valley. Please pretend to be there with me, as we watch Ezekiel being taken on this journey into the valley of the dry bones. **(37:2) "Then He caused me to pass by them all around, and behold, there were very many in the open valley; and indeed they were very dry."**

It was bad enough to be set in the middle of these bones, but now he had to pass by every one of them, to verify that they were very dry. It did not appear to be a pretty sight indeed. After all, who wants to look at all of those bones? Can you visualize them, as you look at them in the spirit with me? Then I could hear God ask him a question, **(vs. 3) "And he said to me, 'Son of man, can these bones live?' So I answered, 'O Lord God, You know.'"** Ezekiel was very wise. He knew that God was waiting for a good answer, so he said, *"O Lord God, You know."* He knew that in his natural mind he could not possibly know how in the world those bones could live. He knew that God had the power to do anything. On my journey in the time capsule, I have seen many things that God has done, so that was the right answer for Ezekiel to say. In my natural mind, it was impossible to believe. In the spiritual mind, I did believe that it was possible.

Those bones were in an open field. They were not buried, so they had hope of a resurrection someday. They represented the house of Israel that was in Babylon and scattered all over the world. God was telling Ezekiel an important message here in this 37th chapter, through the valley of bones. The bones were very dry and scattered, not one of them were in the right place. Then He asked Ezekiel that question, (vs. 3) *"Son of man, can these bones live?"* The very sight of the bones was overwhelming to Ezekiel, but he said, *"O Lord God, You know."* This brings us to the next verse: *(vs. 4) "Again He said to me, 'Prophesy to these bones, and say to them, "O dry bones, hear the word of the Lord!"'"* God could have done it Himself, but He wants to use His servants to perform His will so that they can see His hand working through them. With all of our human reasoning, we would not be able to perform the task of making those bones respond to our command. Nor could Ezekiel, but by being obedient to God's command, it is possible. God was telling Ezekiel to *"Prophesy to these bones, and say to them, 'O dry bones, hear the word of the Lord!'"* This was the first command that God told Ezekiel to do, but He did not stop there. (vs. 5) *"Thus says the Lord God to these bones: 'Surely I will cause breath to inter into you, and you shall live. (vs. 6) I will put sinews on you and bring flesh upon you; and you shall live. Then you shall know that I am the Lord.'"*

With that command from the Lord God, Ezekiel did not waste any time. He began to do what he was told to do. *(vs. 7) "So I prophesied as I was commanded; and as I prophesied, there was a noise, and suddenly a rattling; and the bones came together, bone to bone."* Can you see them coming together with me? Look! Every one of those bones were coming together to form real skeletons. The noise was very terrifying to my ears, sending goose bumps down my legs.

Every bone knew where to go. It was amazing to watch. Ezekiel stood there speechless as the bones came together then, he said **(vs. 8) "Indeed, as I looked, the sinews and the flesh came upon them, and the skin covered them over; but there was no breath in them."** He was surprised that the whole bodies that were formed had no life or breath in them. As he looked around, the Lord God spoke to him once again.

(vs. 9) "Also He said to me, 'Prophesy, son of man, and say to the breath, "Thus says the Lord God: 'Come from the four winds, O breath, and breathe on these slain, that they might live.'"'' O

Lord God, may You breathe on us also that we might be renewed in the spirit, so that we may serve You better! The breath was God's Spirit that came into those new bodies. **(vs. 10) "So I prophesied as He commanded me, and breath came into them, and they lived, and stood upon their feet, an exceedingly great army."** Look all around in the spirit with me. Can you picture this mighty army? What a sight. Ezekiel was totally amazed by this large army.

The amazing thing about this great army was that Ezekiel was not afraid at all. Why? Because he was there in the Spirit, in which there is no fear at all. Then in *Ezekiel 37:11-14,* the Lord God explained to Ezekiel what the bones meant and where this was to take place. **(vs. 11) "Then He said to me, 'Son of man, these bones are the whole house of Israel. They indeed say, "Our bones are dry, our hope is lost, and we ourselves are cut off!"'"** The Lord God is painting a picture here for Ezekiel to understand how things are going to be in the last days, some time during the Tribulation. This is the place that the Lord God will bring all the house of Israel together for this last battle. This is why we had to go back to this time period, so we could understand what was going on. Then the Lord God told Ezekiel **(vs. 12.) "Therefore prophesy and say to them, 'Thus says** the Lord God: "Behold, **O my people, I will open your graves, and cause you to come up from your graves,** and **bring you into the land of Israel.**"""

Can you see what is happening between these two different verses? There is going to be a resurrection some time during the Tribulation period, "*O my people, I will open your graves, and cause you to come up from your graves,*" then the Lord God will "*bring you into the land of Israel.*" *(Ezekiel 37:13, 14) "(vs. 13) Then you shall know that I am the Lord, when I have opened your graves, O My people, and brought you up from your graves. (vs. 14) I will put My Spirit in you, and you shall live, and I will place you in your own land.* **Then you shall know that I, the Lord, have spoken it and performed it, says the Lord.**" Everyone of the house of Israel will be brought back to Israel after the last battle of the Tribulation, even the ones who were in their graves. At that time the Lord God said, (vs. 14) "*I will put My Spirit in you, and you shall live, and I will place you in your own land.*" God's Holy Spirit will come into people more than one time. It happened in the day of Pentecost, it will happen in the very last days also.

God told Ezekiel what was going to happen to His people Israel in the last days. Next Ezekiel, was told how God would take the two nations and join them together to make them into one nation. God said that they would never be divided into two nations again. The key verse is Ezekiel 37:22 "**never" be divided again**; when God joined them together they would not ever be divided, because God's word is steadfast and sure. When God joins something together, nobody nothing can separate them. It would be impossible to do. Not even the devil or principalities could separate them.

I then asked the Lord, "Okay, when is this going to happen?" Many people think that the prophecy was fulfilled when Israel became a nation again in 1967, but that is not true. The things that Ezekiel saw did not happen in the 1967 war or even in our time that we now live in, but it will surely happen in the fourth creation of God, which I have been talking about. During the Tribulation in Revelation, Israel will be scattered all over the nations, but will be brought back to their own land by God at the end of the Tribulation period of time, only this time it will be for ever. So the Lord, through the Holy Spirit, told me to study a little bit closer in Ezekiel for the answers.

Chapter Eleven

THE KINGDOM, ONE KING

P salm 71:20, "You, who have shown me great and severe troubles, Shall revive me again, And bring me up again from the depths of the earth."

King David could hardly wait for this to happen, because he knew that his body would come up out of the grave someday. The Lord talked to Ezekiel again in the next part of the chapter, about how He was going to make Israel into one nation in the land of Israel.

The Lord told Ezekiel something else: **(37:15-17) "Again the word of the Lord came to me, saying, (vs. 16) 'As for you, son of man, take a stick for yourself and write on it: "For <u>Judah and for the children of Israel</u>, his companions." Then take another stick and write on it, "For <u>Joseph, the stick of Ephraim, and for all the house of Israel,</u>**

his companions.'" (vs. 17) Then <u>join them one to</u> <u>another for yourself into one stick, and they will</u> <u>become one in your hand.</u>'"

The Lord uses natural things sometimes to explain spiritual things, because He knows that His children need to see things in the natural realm first before they can understand what is going on in the spiritual realm. The Lord was showing Ezekiel things that were going to happen in the future. The two sticks represented two nations that were separated, but the Lord told Ezekiel **(vs. 17) "Then join them one to** **another for yourself into one stick, and they will** **become one in your hand."** By doing that, the Lord was showing Ezekiel that the two nations were to become one nation. **(vs. 22) "<u>and I will make them</u>** <u>**one nation in the land, on the mountains of Israel**</u>; **and one king shall be king over them all; they shall** **be no longer be two nations, <u>nor shall they ever</u>** <u>**be divided into two kingdoms again.**</u>"

Ezekiel 37:24-25, "<u>David My Servant shall be</u> <u>king over them, and they shall have one shep-</u> <u>herd</u>; they shall also walk in My judgments and observe My statutes, and do them. (vs. 25) Then they shall dwell in the land that I have given to Jacob My servant, where your fathers dwelt; and <u>they shall dwell there</u>, they, their children, and their children's children, forever; and My servant David shall be their prince forever."

"David My Servant shall be king over them." The David in this passage is Jesus Christ because there is only one shepherd, who is the Lord Jesus Christ. When this prophecy takes place, Israel, God's people **"they shall dwell there."** How long will they dwell there? **"forever; and My servant David shall be their prince forever."**

Isaiah 11:1, 2, "There shall come forth a Rod from the stem of Jesse, And a Branch shall grow out of his roots. (vs. 2) The <u>Spirit of the Lord</u> shall rest upon Him, The <u>Spirit of wisdom</u> and <u>understanding</u>, The <u>Spirit of counsel</u> and <u>might</u>, The <u>Spirit of knowledge</u> and the <u>fear of the Lord</u>."

The seven Spirits of God are listed right here: 1. The Spirit of the Lord; 2. The Spirit of wisdom; 3. The Spirit of understanding; 4. The Spirit of counsel; 5. The Spirit of might; 6. The Spirit of knowledge; 7. The fear of the Lord. {Jesus had all of these Spirits resting on Him when He was on the earth.} **(vs. 25) "Then they shall dwell in the land that I have given to Jacob My servant, where your fathers dwelt; and <u>they shall dwell there</u>, they, their children, and their children's children, forever; and My servant David shall be their prince forever."** Here is the secret key to verse 25: "**they shall dwell there.**" How long? "**Forever.**" Now who will be with them? "**My servant David shall be their prince forever.**" Those things are not happening today in our duration, so this is a future thing that will happen, during the thousand-year reign. Can you see key secrets here?

The Lord was showing Ezekiel all of these things by painting a picture of them in his spirit so that he could write them down. The Lord was setting the atmosphere in motion by letting Ezekiel know that God was going to make this happen, because in the next few verses He explained something about a covenant to Ezekiel that He was going to fulfill.

37:26, "Moreover I will make a covenant of peace with them, and it shall be an everlasting covenant with them; I will establish them and multiply them, and I will set My sanctuary in their midst forevermore."

{The covenant that the anti-Christ made was broken during the great Tribulation, so God was telling Ezekiel that His covenant would never be broken.} God said, "**I will,**" three times in this verse alone. Speaking something three times means something. If God said it, He will perform what He said He would do. God told Ezekiel three things: **First:** He was going to "**make a covenant of peace.**" It would be an: "**everlasting** covenant," there will be no end of it. **Second:** He said that He was going to: "**... establish them and multiply them.**" This means that they were going to keep having children. **Third: "I will set My sanctuary in their midst forevermore."**

The key secret verse: "<u>**I will set My sanctuary in their midst forevermore**</u>." Again, God is painting another picture here for Ezekiel to remember; "**I will set My sanctuary in their midst forevermore.**" It is so important that God says it again in the next verse: **37:27, "<u>My tabernacle also shall be with them;</u> indeed I will be their God, and they shall be My people, (vs. 28) The nations also will know that I, the Lord, sanctify Israel, <u>when My sanctuary is in their midst forevermore.</u>"** By this time, Ezekiel was probably on the edge of his seat, waiting to hear when this was going to happen. I, too, was waiting to hear when it was going to happen. There were some pretty strong statements made here to Ezekiel. God Himself had spoken to him by His Spirit. I am glad that I have not read too many books about this subject, because then my mind would not have been open as much for the Holy Spirit to teach me on these things.

Now that God had those things imbedded in Ezekiel's spirit, He was about to say some things that had to take place before those things we just read could take place.

God was going to take Ezekiel in the Spirit to a place in the far future, into the book of Revelation. That was one hard book for me to understand. How about you? But for me to understand what was going on in Ezekiel, I needed to go there to be able to understand what was going to happen with Ezekiel's visions.

There are **key secrets** in this next Chapter that will help us to understand what Ezekiel was talking about in this chapter. If I would miss any one of these **key secrets**, my understanding would be limited on its content. Keep in mind that the battle I am going to take you to a battle that is to be fought in the future, way beyond our time. It will be fought at the end of the great Tribulation, spoken of by John in the book of Revelation. **First**: I will show you things that Ezekiel saw in the Spirit, so I will only be able to show you what the Holy Spirit has shown to me. This Fourth Creation of God is by far a hard one for me to show anyone its existence, but by God's grace, the Holy Spirit has opened my spirit's mind to be able to help me see the fourth creation, in the Spirit, by His marvelous teaching through the word of God.

Ezekiel 38:1-4, 9, "Now the word of the Lord came to me, saying, (vs. 2.) 'Son of man, set your face against <u>Gog, of the land of Magog,</u>

the prince of Rosh, Meshech, and Tubal, prophesy against him, and say, "Thus says the Lord God: 'Behold, I am against you, O Gog, the prince of Rosh, Meshech, and Tubal. (vs. 4) I will turn you around, put hooks into your jaws, and lead you out, with all your army, horses and horsemen, all splendidly clothed, a great company with bucklers and shields, all of them handling swords.'" <u>(vs. 9)</u> <u>"You will ascend, coming like a storm, covering the land like a cloud, you and all of your troops and many peoples with you."</u>

God told Ezekiel, all about this great battle of the future in Chapters 37-39. I do not want to write them all down, but you can read them for yourself. I just want to highlight some of them for you now. Ezekiel was given a vision of the last battle of the great Tribulation. I will show you that in the next chapter.

"ON THAT DAY IT SHALL COME TO PASS"

Ezekiel 38:10, "Thus says the Lord God: '<u>On that day it shall come to pass </u>that thought will arise in your mind, and you will make an evil plan.'" The Lord prophesied that there was coming a certain day in the future, when His armies would defeat the armies of the devil, or in this case, Gog and his armies that were led by Satan. In verse 14, the same phrase is used again: **"On that day." Ezekiel 38:14-16, "Therefore, son of man, prophesy and say, 'Thus says the Lord God: "<u>On that day when My people Israel dwell safely, will you not know it?</u> (vs. 15) Then you will come from your place out of the far north, you and many peoples with you, all of them <u>riding on horses, a great company and a mighty army</u>. (vs. 16) <u>You will come up against My people Israel like a cloud, to cover the land. It will be in the latter days that I will bring you against My land,</u> so that the nations may know Me, when I am hallowed in you, <u>O Gog</u>, before their eyes."'"** This one is the first battle against Israel at the end of the Tribulation. Then at the same time this one takes place, God is going to place a judgment on Gog:

JUDGMENT ON GOG

Great judgment from God will fall on Gog and everyone who sides with him. Look at these next few verses in **Ezekiel 38:18-22:**

(v. 18) "'And it will come to pass at the same time, <u>when Gog comes against the land of Israel</u>,' says the Lord God, 'that My fury will show in My face. (vs. 19) For in My jealousy and in <u>the fire of My wrath</u> I have spoken: Surely in <u>that day</u> there shall be a <u>great earthquake</u> in the land of Israel, (vs. 20) so that the <u>fish</u> of the sea, the <u>birds</u> of the heavens, the <u>beast</u> of the field, <u>all creeping things</u> that creep on the earth, and all men who are on the face of the earth <u>shall shake at My presence.</u> The mountains shall be thrown down, the steep places shall fall, and every wall shall fall to the ground. (vs. 21) <u>I will call for a sword against Gog</u> throughout all My Mountains,' says the Lord God. Every man's sword will be against his brother. (vs. 22) And <u>I will bring him to judgment with pestilence and bloodshed</u>; I will rain down on him, on his troops, and on the many peoples who are with him, flooding rain, great hailstones, fire, and brimstone. (vs. 23) Thus I will magnify Myself and sanctify Myself, and I will be known in the eyes of many nations. Then they shall know that I am the Lord.'"

This battle was very bad, as you can see, but God was not done yet, because in the next chapter God told Ezekiel to prophesy against Gog again, with more bad news, that God is going to make supper for the **birds** and the **beast** of the fields.

Ezekiel 39:1-3, "And you, son of man, prophesy against Gog, and say, 'Thus says the Lord God; "Behold, <u>I am against you,, O Gog</u>, the prince of Rosh, Meshech, and Tubal; (vs. 2) and I will <u>turn you around</u> and lead you on, bringing you up from the far north, and <u>bring you against the mountains of Israel</u>. (vs. 3) Then <u>I will knock the bow out of your left hand, and cause the arrows to fall out of your right hand.</u>"'"

Our God is a wonderful God. Look what He is going to do unto Gog! **First**, He is going to turn him around, then He will bring Gog and company against the *mountains of Israel.* **Secondly**, He will knock the bow right out their hands, causing *the arrows to fall out of your right hand.* They are not going to know what hit them when this happens. I like this battle already. Can you see their faces with me when that happens? Gog and all of his friends will be helpless all of a sudden. Then God said through this prophesy: **(vs. 4) "You shall fall upon the mountains of Israel, you and your troops and the peoples who are with you; I will** give you to <u>birds of prey of every sort and to the beast of the field</u> to be devoured. (vs. 5) You shall fall on the open field; for I have spoken," says the Lord God. The battle is now going to get even worse because Ezekiel, through the prophecy, tells them that they shall fall upon the *"mountains of Israel."* Then he says that the birds and beast are going to feast on them. Finally, **(vs. 6) "And I will send fire on Magog and on those who live in security in the coastlands. Then they shall know that I am the Lord."** God let them know that no one was going to escape His wrath. In His final good by to them, He said, **(vs. 8) "'surely it is coming, and it shall be done,' says the Lord God. <u>'This is the day of which I have spoken.'"</u>** Here is the explanation of, "On that day." God gave the very day that He was talking about in this key secret verse. **<u>"This is the day of which I have spoken."</u>** This is the same "day" that John saw in a vision in Revelation 19.

JOHN'S VISION OF **<u>"THAT DAY"</u>**

THE DAY THE BEAST AND HIS ARMIES ARE DEFEATED.

First I must show you something that happens after the fall of Babylon at the end of the great Tribulation. *Revelation 19:6, "And I heard, as* *it were, the voice of a great multitude, as the sound of mighty thundering, saying, 'Alleluia! For the Lord God Omnipotent reigns!'"*

Can you hear this great announcement? *"For the Lord God Omnipotent reigns!"* **God is setting the atmosphere for His coming to the earth, that His prophecy is coming to pass "on that day." Something great is going to happen that we have been waiting for a long time!** *19:7, 8, "(vs. 7) 'Let us be glad and rejoice and give Him glory, for the <u>marriage of the Lamb has come, and His wife has made herself ready.</u>' (vs. 8) And to her it was granted to be arrayed in fine linen, clean and bright, for the fine linen is the righteous acts of the saints."* **The greatest marriage is now going to take place. Are you ready for it? It will happen at this time in the future in "one day." I can hardly wait for it to take place! John said something very important in the next verse:** *(vs. 9) "Then he said to me, 'write: "Blessed are those who are called to the <u>marriage supper of the Lamb!</u>"' And he said to me, 'These are the true sayings of God.'"*

PART TWO

THE REVELATION OF THE THINGS TO COME

Chapter Twelve

THE SECOND COMING

Is there a rapture of the Church? It is time to look at what God says about it. I did study it in depth, in *1 Corinthians 4:13-18*, also *5:1-11.* There are key verses that may bring some light on this subject. First of all, I am going to pray for God's wisdom so that I might know the truth by His standards, not by what the world thinks. I started this study on the second coming on 10/15/12, and I finished it on 6/25/13. It is very important that I know the whole truth on this matter, so that I will not lead any of my followers in the wrong direction.

My prayer: "Dear heavenly Father, I come to You in the name of Jesus Your Son. I pray for wisdom as well as understanding as I study your word. I pray that You would open my spiritual ears that I might hear the voice of Your Holy Spirit, I pray that You would open my spiritual eyes that I might see into the spiritual realm so that I might receive a revelation of Your Holy Word, so that I can know the complete truth that is in Your word. Help me to study your word by revelation from the greatest teacher of all, the Holy Spirit. Block out any distractions from my mind, even the teaching of man, that are not of you. Soften my heart to receive the seed of your word, prepare my heart so that your seed of the word can grow, that it will bear much fruit. Thank You, Lord, for hearing my prayer. Amen."

This is a beginning of a new day in my life, where I want to study the word of God to the best of my ability, so that I will not be ashamed at His coming back to the earth. Look at the key phrase, "The Day of the Lord." It has great meaning on this subject. "The Day of the Lord," is mentioned many times in the word of God. I am going to study about the "Day of the Lord."

The earth is in labor pains right now. All of God's creations are waiting for the redemption of the earth, for the earth will be restored like never before. The Lord has promised to come back two times in His word. The first time, He is going to come in the clouds to meet all of His chosen saints in the air; what we call the rapture of the Church. When He comes back the second time to the earth, it will be to defeat the beast, then to bind up Satan for a period of 1,000 years, then He will rule and reign with His saints for at least 1,000 years. The mystery of the future belongs to those whom God calls His children! The Lord through the Holy Spirit has shown to me many things that pertain to the future. There are many things that I have not seen before. Again, He has blown my little mind with things that opened up my mind with new understanding, into the spiritual realm of understanding, way beyond my natural way of thinking.

Get ready for a journey into the future, where you will be able to see things you may not have seen before. The first thing I want you to look at is the phrase: "The Day of the Lord." Revelation talks about this day, as well as the Old Testament and New Testaments prophets and saints. *Isaiah 2:11, 12, "(vs. 11) And the Lord alone shall be exalted* **in that day**. *(vs. 12) For* **the day of the Lord** *of hosts shall come upon everything proud and lofty."* Isaiah was talking about a special day of the Lord in these verses. In this particular day, the Lord shall be exalted alone. To learn more about this day, I knew that I needed more scriptures to read. *Isaiah 13:6, "Wail. For* **the day of the Lord** *is at hand! It* **will come as destruction** *from the Almighty."* Again, Isaiah mentions a special day of the Lord, where there will be destruction.

Ezekiel 30:3, "For the day is near, Even **the day of the Lord** is near; <u>It will be a day of clouds, the time of the Gentiles."</u> (This part could be talking about the Rapture. Just a thought.)

Joel 6:15, "Alas for the day! For **the day of the Lord** is at hand; <u>It shall come as destruction from the Almighty."</u> Joel gives a lot of detail in the rest of the verses in this chapter. Joel was given the same word as Isaiah 13:6. They are talking about the same day of the Lord, as I have just seen from these scriptures. Then the prophet Joel goes on to say something else about the day of the Lord in *2:30,* "And <u>I will show wonders in the heaven and in the earth</u>: Blood and fire and pillars of smoke. (vs. 31) The sun shall be turned into darkness, And the moon into blood, Before the coming of the great and awesome **day of the Lord**."

I must move on to my brother, the prophet Amos, who also spoke of the day of the Lord: *Amos 5:16,* "Therefore the Lord God of hosts, the Lord, says this: <u>'There shall be wailing in all streets,</u> And they shall say in all the highways, "Alas! Alas!" They shall call the farmer to mourning, And skillful lamenters to wailing. (vs. 17) In all vineyards there shall be wailing, For I will pass through you,' Says the Lord. (vs. 18) A **day of trumpet and alarm** Against the fortified cities And *against the high towers.'"* And he goes on to tell more, but I will let you read the rest on your own.

Malachi 4:5, "Behold, <u>I will send you Elijah the prophet</u> Before the coming of **the great and dreadful day of the Lord.** *(vs. 6) And he will turn The hearts of the fathers to the children, And the hearts of the children to their fathers, Lest I come and strike the earth with a curse."*

Acts 2:20, "The sun shall be turned into darkness, And the moon into blood, Before the coming of the great and **awesome day of the Lord***."*

1 Corinthians 5:5, "deliver such a one to Satan for the destruction of the flesh that his spirit may be saved in **the day of the Lord Jesus."**

2 Corinthians 1:14, "(as also you have understood us in part), that we are your boast as you also are ours, in **the day of the Lord Jesus."**

2 Peter 3:10, "But **the day of the Lord** <u>*will come as a thief in the night,*</u> *in which the heavens will pass away with a great noise, and the elements will melt with fervent heat; both the earth and the works that are in it will be burned up."* "The day of the Lord" in all of these scriptures refers to the book of Revelation, which is the revelation of our Lord. Whether it is one twenty-four-hour day or many days is not the question. By that I mean, this day of the Lord is His day of being revealed as King of Kings and Lord of Lords. In this day of the Lord, the kingdoms of this world shall become His kingdom, as it is revealed in the book of Revelation.

As revealed in the previous scriptures, there are many things that will take place in that day of the Lord. 1. The Lord alone will be exalted. 2. That day will come as destruction. 3. It will be a day of clouds, the time of the Gentiles. 4. It will be a day of wonders. Blood, fire, pillars of smoke, the sun will be darkness, and the moon will be as blood. 5. There will be wailing in the streets. 6. It will be a day of trumpet and alarm. 7. I will send Elijah before that day. 8. Peter 3:10, "the day of the Lord will come as a thief in the night."

THE SECOND COMING OF CHRIST ON THE CLOUDS

Matthew 24:29-31, (vs. 29) "**Immediately after the tribulation of those days** *the sun will be darkened, and the moon will not give its light; the stars will fall from heaven, and the powers of the heavens will be shaken.* **(vs. 30) Then the signs of the Son of Man will appear in heaven,** *and then all the tribes of the earth will mourn, and* **they will see the Son of Man coming on the clouds of heaven** *with power* *and great glory. (vs. 31) And* **He will send His angles with a great sound of a trumpet, and they will gather together His elect from the four winds, from one end of heaven to the other.**"

I have been instructed to study about the second coming of Christ. I want to know my Lord in an even deeper way, so that I can know when He is coming back to the earth. Then I want to know if the Church will be taken out of the earth before the great Tribulation or in the middle of it, or after the great Tribulation. It is my intension to study this subject by letting the Spirit of God teach me, instead of man's teaching.

"Holy Spirit of God, I pray in the name of Jesus that you teach me according to your ways, so that I can know the truth. Amen."

I have been taught that the fourth chapter of Thessalonians was talking about the Rapture of the Church, so right now I am going to study this fourth chapter in a new way, forgetting my old teaching for now, so that I can study it by listening to what the Spirit is speaking about on this subject.

1 Thessalonians 4:13, "But I do not want you to be ignorant, brethren, concerning those who have fallen asleep, lest you sorrow as others who have no hope. (vs. 14) For if we believe that Jesus died and rose again, even so God will bring with Him those who sleep in Jesus. (vs. 15) For this we say to you by the word of the Lord, that we who are alive and remain until **the coming of the Lord** *will by no means precede those who are asleep. (vs. 16) For the* **Lord Himself will descend from heaven** *with a shout, with the voice of an archangel, and with the* **trumpet of God.** *And the dead in Christ will rise first. (vs. 17) Then we who are alive and remain shall be caught up together with them in the clouds to meet the Lord in the air. And thus we shall always be with the Lord. (vs. 18) Therefore comfort one another with these words.*

Our dear brother Paul was the author of 1 Thessalonians. I believe that there is a **key verses** in these verses above that might shed some light on the subject of the catching up of the Church, commonly known as the Rapture of the Church. It took me a long time to put these things in order, but with the help of the Holy Spirit I was able to get it done. Again, while I was doing this study, I did not use any other books or commentaries. All I used was the word of

God, directed by the Holy Spirit. The first thing Paul wanted his readers to know was not to be ignorant: *1 Thessalonians 4:13, "But* **I do not want you to be ignorant,** *brethren, concerning those who have fallen asleep."* Paul wanted his followers to have an understanding that all believers will someday be caught up to meet Christ in the air. When will this happen? *(vs. 15) "For this we say to you by the word of the Lord, that we who are alive and remain until* **the coming of the Lord** *will by no means precede those who are asleep."* The first key in this verse that gives us a clue when this event is going to take place: "**the coming of the Lord,**" the Lord Jesus is coming back again. Now it is up to us to find out when this is going to happen. Paul tells his followers that those who are alive when Jesus comes back will not be changed before those who have already died. By looking at the next verse, I will show you more key words that will give you an understanding of when it will take place. *(vs. 16) "For the* **Lord Himself will descend from heaven** *with a shout, with the voice of an archangel, and with the* **trumpet of God.** *And the dead in Christ will rise first."*

Jesus will "**descend from heaven**" with a special instrument: "*the* **trumpet of God.**" Paul then said that the "*dead in Christ will rise first.*" There is going to be a resurrection of the dead, which by the way, is the first resurrection. I will show you that right now. Look in Revelation with me with an open mind, so that the Holy Spirit can give you the wisdom of understanding. To set the stage, the second coming of Christ is going to take place in the middle of the great Tribulation period. Then He shall descend from heaven, at which time the dead in Christ shall come back from the dead, then we who are alive shall meet up in the air, with all of them and with the Lord.

(vs. 17) "Then **we who are alive and remain shall be caught up together with** *them in the clouds to meet the Lord in the air. And thus we shall always be with the Lord."* There is going to be two resurrections of the dead. In the first part of the next scripture, John says that **the rest of the dead will not live again until after the one thousand-year** reign. They will be a part of the second resurrection, which takes place at the Great White Throne Judgment in Revelation 20. Then in (vs., John talks about the first resurrection, which will happen at the first appearance of Christ in the clouds, as we will read later on. This first resurrection is what I call the Rapture of the Churcn. Now look in Revelation 20:5, 6: *(vs. 5) "But the rest of the dead did not live again until the thousand years were finished.* **This is the first resurrection**. *(vs. 6)* **Blessed and holy is he who has part in**

the first resurrection. *Over such the second death has no power, but they shall be priest of God and of Christ, and shall reign with Him a thousand years."* This will take place during the fourth creation of God.

I am talking about the second coming of Christ on the clouds. He does not come back to the earth at this time. This second coming of Christ is what we call the Rapture of the Church. When Jesus ascended to heaven on the clouds, He also said that He would return on the clouds. That is why it is called the second coming of Christ. Then at the end of the great Tribulation, Christ descends from heaven to do battle with the beast and false prophets. Jesus predicted this second coming while He was here on this earth. I had a hard time with these things myself on this concept of the Rapture that we just studied, because the old teaching about the Rapture of the Church said that the Rapture of the Church was going to take place before the great Tribulation. This is why I had to put aside my former teaching to allow the Holy Spirit to teach me the truth of His word. I truly want the Rapture to take place before the Tribulation. I hope it does, but I also want to know the truth of what God is trying to teach me. Either way, I know that I am ready to meet Him in the air when He returns. Now in Revelation 20:6 that we just read, John explains that those who were a part of the first resurrection are the ones who "*shall reign with Him a thousand years.*" When did that occur? When Christ appears on a white horse in Revelation 19:11, all of us will follow Him on white horses to battle the beast. Then Christ will bind up Satan for 1,000 years. There are key secrets within these verses that will help us to understand the teachings of Christ. There is much wisdom in the word of God, but it requires one to seek it like a buried treasure. The scriptures are scattered throughout the Bible on many subjects, so they must be put together with precession, somewhat like a puzzle. There are too many people who take different scriptures out of context to satisfy their own desires.

But to find the true meaning of these scriptures, one is to ask the greatest teacher of all time for the correct answers. That person is the Holy Spirit. Back to Matthew 24, Matthew gives some clues as what things are going to take place before Christ is seen in the clouds. Notice nowhere within those verses is there any mention of Christ touching down on the earth at that time. Look at (vs. 30): "*Then the sign of the Son of Man will appear in heaven, and then all the tribes of the earth will mourn, and they will see the Son of Man coming on the clouds of heaven with power and great glory.*" But then John stops there, because Christ is not coming back to set up His kingdom on earth at that time. No, not at all, because in the next verse he goes on to say, (*vs. 31*) *"And He will send His angels with a great sound of a trumpet, and they will gather together His elect from the four winds, from one end of heaven to the other."*

Another key secret is in Matthew's next writings that follow. Jesus tells five parables about His coming. They are written in parables so that the foolish ones could not understand what He meant. In these parables, He is specific about the fact that some will be taken away in the Rapture, and some would be left. The Holy Spirit took me to another passage of scripture in *1 Corinthians 15:50-55: (vs. 50) "Now this I say, brethren, that flesh and blood cannot inherit the kingdom of God; nor does corruption inherit incorruption. (vs. 51) Behold, <u>I tell you a mystery: We shall not all sleep, but we shall all be changed- (vs. 52) in a moment, in the twinkling of an eye,</u> **at the last trumpet**. For the **trumpet will sound**, and the <u>dead will be raised incorruptible, and we shall be changed.</u> (vs. 53) For this corruptible must put on incorruption, and this mortal must put on immortality. (vs. 54) So when this corruptible has put on incorruption, and this mortal has put on immortality, then shall be brought to pass the saying that is written: "Death is swallowed up* *in victory.*" These scriptures in 1 Corinthians 15:50-55 are talking about the first resurrection that will take place when Christ comes back in the clouds of heaven. That may surprise you, but there are only two resurrections talked about in the scriptures other than when Jesus was raised from the dead. I have talked about these things earlier. I needed to show you that 1 Corinthians 15 is talking about the first main resurrection of the believers, which had to take place after the resurrection of our Lord. 1Thessalonians also fits into the same period of time, because it talks about the day of the Lord also.

1 Thessalonians 5:2, "For **you yourselves know perfectly that the day of the Lord so comes as a thief in the night."** The day of the Lord will come as a surprise to those who are not looking for Him. He will come just like a thief comes into one's home, taking what he wants before the people in the house realize what hit them. This first appearance of Christ coming on the clouds of heaven is when the Rapture of the Church will take place. By reading these scriptures, everything so far looks like it is going to happen after the first half of the Tribulation, according to this study. Paul knows very well about "the day of the Lord," because in the next chapter he expounds on that day. It is not just an ordinary day, but "the day of the Lord."

It is a day of His return to the earth, to rule the earth during the 1,000-years reign, with all of His saints, who, by the way, will be in their new glorified bodies that were changed during Christ's first return on the clouds of heaven. *Matthew 24:31, "And He will send His angels with a great sound of a trumpet, and they will gather together His elect from the four winds, from one end of heaven to the other."*

The Lord Jesus is going to send His angels to do one last task before He touches His feet on the Mount of Olives, or the seven bowls of wrath are poured out. The Lord will send His angels with a special trumpet that is very loud. The sounding of this seventh trumpet will do more than one thing: this trumpet will set into motion many things. Now these verses are very clear as to when Christ is coming back in the clouds, don't you think? First, in (vs. 29), He tells us that He is coming right after the first half of the great Tribulation of those days: **(vs. 29) "Immediately after the tribulation of those days.**" Something happens next. What can you see? Now remember, the great Tribulation lasts for seven years, so the time of His return in the clouds could be determined by key secret verses that follow, since there are many days in the great Tribulation period. **(vs. 30) "Then the signs of the Son of Man will appear in heaven."** When is Christ coming? Can you see Him coming? **"They will see the Son of Man coming on the clouds of heaven."** I was surprised when I read these things! But now I see, because Jesus spoke these words in Matthew, they are true. The first appearing of Christ is for what we call the Rapture. With that being said, I needed to look a little bit closer at what the scriptures are saying. I knew that I must listen to what the Spirit of God was saying to me.

Matthew 24:27, "For as lightning that comes from the east is visible even in the west, so will be the coming of the Son of Man." What was Matthew trying to say here? As surely as you can see the effects of lightning, you will see the effects of Christ's return. I am amazed when I see a good lightning storm. Not one of them is the same, but all of them are able to get my attention because of their brightness. Matthew was saying to us, "You will not miss seeing Christ's return in the clouds because He will have your attention, just like lightning gets your attention." If you can see the lightning, you will see Christ coming in the clouds. It will be brighter than lightning, because Jesus is the Light of the world.

Matthew 24:28, "Wherever there is a carcass, there the vultures will gather." Again, Matthew uses this example of a carcass and vultures as a way of communication, saying that just as it is a fact if there is a carcass lying dead, there will be vultures there also, so when you see the things taking place in the end times as described by the scriptures, you can rest assured that Christ will soon return in the clouds. Matthew then goes on to tell about His return by saying, "Here are the signs:" (*vs. 29*) *"Immediately after the distress of those days 'the sun will be darkened, and the moon will not give its light; the stars will fall from the sky, and the heavenly bodies will be shaken.'"* So now I needed to know which days of the great Tribulation Matthew was talking about. I needed to look for the key verses or secret codes that are outlined in the Bible that would explain these things about the second coming of Christ Jesus. He speaks it very clearly in *Matthew 24:30* "**(vs. 30) Then the signs of the Son of Man will appear in heaven,** *and then all the tribes of the earth will mourn, and* **they will see the Son of Man coming on the clouds of heaven** *with power and great glory. (vs. 31) And* **He will send His angels with a great sound of a trumpet, and they will gather together His elect from the four winds, from one end of heaven to the other.**"

The second coming of the Lord will take place in the sky on the clouds. He is not going to come upon the earth at this time. No, He is coming on the clouds to meet all of His saints, in verse 31. He sends His angels to gather together His elect first, then the dead in Christ, then every believer who is alive at that time, then every one of these will be caught up to meet Jesus in the air on the clouds, to be with the Lord forever. Look at these next scriptures again to see how they go together.

1 Thessalonians 4:13, "But I do not want you to be ignorant, brethren, concerning those who have fallen asleep, lest you sorrow as others who have no hope. (vs. 14) For if we believe that Jesus died and rose again, even so God will bring with Him those who sleep in Jesus. (vs. 15) For this we say to you by the word of the Lord, that we who are alive and remain until **the coming of the Lord** *will by no means precede those who are asleep. (vs. 16) For the* **Lord Himself will descend from heaven** *with a shout, with the voice of an archangel, and with the* **trumpet of God.** *And the dead in Christ will rise first. (vs. 17) Then we who are alive and remain shall be caught up together with them in the clouds to meet the Lord in the air. And thus we shall always be with the Lord. (vs. 18) Therefore comfort one another with these words."*

This second coming of the Lord Jesus is outlined very clearly as to when this event is going to happen. 1Thessalonians is an extension of Matthew 24; they both go hand-in-hand. I never saw these things before until the Spirit of God opened my eyes. He showed me **key words** that brought understanding to my spiritual mind. God's elect in these scriptures are not just the 144,000 saints who were sealed by God, as some teach. No, not at all, but the elect of God are all of the ones who were listed in these scriptures. All of these things happen in the sky. They will not return to the earth until Christ comes back to the earth, riding on a white horse with all of His saints in Revelation 19. So there are two second comings of Christ Jesus. The first one is what I just talked about. The reason they are both called the second coming of Christ is that when Christ Jesus left the earth, He left on the clouds. He said that He would return the same way, on the clouds. He did not say that He would touch back down on the earth at that time. Now that makes His second coming accurate concerning the clouds. Now concerning the other second coming of Christ Jesus, His second coming to the earth will be when He comes back to the earth as described in Revelation 19:11-16. He will take over the earth at this time, then rule and reign with His saints for 1,000 years.

There we have it. Both times His second coming is defined: one in the clouds, one on the earth. Both times it is His second coming. I was always taught that the coming of the Lord would take place before the great Tribulation, but now I know they were wrong, because of what Jesus Himself said in Matthew 24.

Note: There are **three key words** that should be considered when studying the scriptures. They are: **1.** where did the event take place? **2**. When did it happen? **3.** How did it take place?

Matthew 24:29-31, (vs.29) "**Immediately after the tribulation of those days** *the sun will be darkened, and the moon will not give its light; the stars will fall from heaven, and the powers of the heavens will be shaken.* **(vs. 30) Then the signs of the Son of Man will appear in heaven,** *and then all the tribes of the earth will mourn, and* **they will see the Son of Man coming on the clouds of heaven** *with power and great glory. (vs. 31) And* **He will send His angels with a great sound of a trumpet, and they will gather together His elect from the four winds, from one end of heaven to the other.**"

I am looking for key verses or secret codes that will unlock the mystery of Revelation. *(vs. 29)* "**Immediately after the tribulation of those days** *the sun will be darkened, and the moon will not give its light; the stars will fall from heaven, and the powers of the heavens will be shaken."* {**Matthew is talking about the first half of the great Tribulation, or three-and-a-half years.**}

What takes place right after the Tribulation? 1. "*The sun will be darkened*" 2. "*Moon will not give its light*" 3. "*The stars will fall from heaven*" 4. "*The powers of the heavens will be shaken.*" Where in the scriptures does this happen, pertaining to the Tribulation?

Daniel 7:13, 14, (vs. 13) "I was watching in the night visions, And behold, **One like the Son of Man, Coming with the clouds of heaven!** *He came to the Ancient of Days, And they brought Him near before Him. (vs. 14 Then* **to Him was given dominion and glory and a kingdom,** *That all people, nations, and languages should serve Him. His dominion is an ever-lasting dominion,* **Which shall not pass away**, *And His kingdom the one Which shall not be destroyed."* Daniel was given the vision of the coming of the Lord! Daniel just confirmed that the coming of the Lord he saw was the same as what Matthew and Paul saw in their visions concerning the coming of the Lord.

Daniel was telling us that when the Lord comes in the clouds, *"He came to the Ancient of Days, And they brought Him near before Him."* It was then at that time God the Father gave Jesus the kingdom of the earth. Everything is always established in heaven first before it takes place on the earth. This kingdom would start in the Fourth Creation of God, according to the Prophet Ezekiel. All of the details are in the following chapters in this book.

Chapter Thirteen

THE SECOND COMING ACCORDING TO REVELATION

The book of Revelation is a book of mysteries. There are symbols, **key secret verses, codes, and numbers.** I am studying it for the purpose of establishing when the Second coming of Christ is, not the day or hour, but the order of events. John was given the task to write the things he saw happen. Not necessarily the exact order in which they will happen, when that time comes. I found myself scratching my head when I read this great book. It is like no other book that I have ever read. I do not claim to know all of its contents because it would take a long time to do that. Even then, I do not think any one person could know everything about its content either. When I study any scriptures in the Bible, especially on a particular subject, I try to place myself with the characters of who I am reading about, as though I was right there with them, because this helps me to know what they are talking about.

For instance, in the book of Revelation, I try to see myself with John by allowing myself to be in the Spirit, so that I can visualize in the Spirit what John saw. Sounds crazy, so try it some time for yourself? I am usually very surprised at the results. It is kind of like being a private investigator in real life. Do you agree? If you have never tried to study that way, you probably will not answer yes to that question.

Revelation 1:9, "I John, both your brother and companion in the tribulation and kingdom and patience of Jesus Christ, was on the island that is called Patmos for the word of God and for the testimony of Jesus Christ. (vs. 10) I was in the Spirit on the Lord's Day, and I heard behind me a loud voice, as of a trumpet, (vs. 11) saying, 'I am the Alpha and the Omega, the First and the Last,' and, 'What you see, write in a book and send it to the seven churches which are in Asia: to Ephesus, to Smyrna, to Pergamos, to Thyatira, to Sardis, to Philadelphia, and to Laodicea.'"

Even though John was stuck on the island, he did not blame God for his imprisonment. Not at all. He knew that he was there for a reason, so he continued to be in the Spirit of prayer and worship in God's presence. God put John there so that he would not be distracted from all of the things that were going on, especially with the church being persecuted in his day. It was a place where John was pretty much alone, except for the guards. Therefore the prison bars were his only companions. God had an assignment for John, to write. Yes, it was one of the most important books of the Bible. The Lord Jesus chose John to be the very one to whom He could reveal His secret revelation of Himself. Also the Lord used John to be the chosen one, to be the one He could show what was going to take place in the last days.

The Lord revealed to John His very being. He also revealed the garments that He wore. Then the Lord told him what to write by starting with the seven churches, then what their condition was. The first three chapters were devoted to the condition of the churches. He was shown their condition, which would bring judgment if they did not repent. In chapter four, John was invited up to heaven, to see what was going to take place. *Revelation 4:1, "After these things I looked, and behold, a door standing open in heaven. And the first voice which I heard was like a trumpet speaking with me, saying,* **'Come up here, and I will show you things which must take place after this.'"** By this time, John must have been overwhelmed at the things he had already seen, but by being in the Spirit, he had strength to go beyond his human reasoning. So far, John, saw that God's judgment on the earth was going to start with the seven churches.

After that, John was called up to take a trip into heaven. (Rev.4:1) *"Come up here, and I will show you things which must take place after this."* What an honor that was for John to receive an invitation into heaven itself. I do not know how far it is to get to heaven, but John got there immediately. This calling to come up to heaven was for John only, because he was the only one to whom the Lord spoke. To assume this was the Rapture of the Church would not be an accurate statement, because this was the Lord calling one individual, which was John. John was called to be the Lord's servant. His task was to take notes, then he was to write what things were told to him or what things he saw, but there were things that he was not to write also. John saw the throne of the Lord with twenty-four other thrones that had twenty-four elders setting on them. He saw seven lamps of fire burning before the throne. He saw four living creatures full of eyes in front and in back.

I am not going to try to say anything about these creatures except what John saw. There are those who say that these creatures are something else or represent other things. This is not my purpose. All I know for sure is that when they do certain things, people fall on their knees. Revelation *4:9, "Whenever the living creatures give glory and honor and thanks to Him who sits on the throne, who lives forever, (vs. 10) the twenty-four elders fall down before Him who sits on the throne and worship Him who lives forever and ever, and cast their crowns before the throne, saying:"* These living creatures are mentioned more than one time. I believe they are real living creatures, as stated in John's writings. John is getting an overview of the things that are going to happen in the last days, in the great Tribulation period. Everything he saw will happen some time during the great Tribulation, but not in the particular order in which he saw them. They will take place in God's order of perfection. In the fifth chapter of Revelation, John was able to see other things happen that he was not to record.

In (Rev. 5:1, he saw a scroll that had writing on the inside and back, which was sealed with seven seals. Then he saw the one who could open it; it was the Lamb. The Lamb had seven horns and seven eyes: *(vs. 6) "which are the seven Spirits of God sent out into all the earth."* I often wondered how God could see everything in the world, at the same time. These seven Spirits of God go throughout the whole earth at record speeds. There is nowhere we can hide from Him, because He is everywhere.

THE SEVEN SEALS WRITTEN ON THE SCROLL

John saw what was written on the scroll. It was revealed to him by the Lamb, in the 6th chapter of Revelation. Six seals were revealed to him. The **first seal,** there was a **white horse**; the one who sat on it (*vs. 2) "went out* **conquering and to conquer**.*"* The **second seal,** another **horse, fiery red,** went out to **take peace from the earth**; verses 3, 4. Next John was invited to see the **third seal** opened, in which he saw the **third horse,** a **black horse**, and the one who sat on it had a pair of scales in his hand. Then John was invited to see the **fourth seal** opened: *(Rev. 6:8) "So I looked, and behold, a pale horse. And the name of him who sat on it was Death, and Hades followed with him. And power was given to them over a fourth of the earth, to kill with the sword, with hunger, with death, and by the beasts of the earth."*

The first four seals were just the beginning of the earth's judgment. Much more shall take place during the Tribulation. The first seal, a conquering rider was going through the earth. The second seal, a rider on the fiery red horse took away peace from the earth.

The third seal, the rider brought problems of financial unrest to the earth. Finally, the **fourth seal,** the rider on the pale horse brought war with swords, hunger, and death by the beasts of the earth. The **fifth seal** was devoted to the martyrs of the Tribulation. Everybody just thinks that we Christians are not going to be a part of the Tribulation troubles, so I was instructed to look at this fifth seal a little bit closer.

Revelation 6:9, "When He opened the **fifth seal***, I saw under the alter the* **souls of those who had been slain for the word of God and for the testimony which they held***. (vs. 10) And they cried with a loud voice, saying, 'How long, O Lord, holy and true, until You judge and avenge our blood on those who dwell on the earth?' (vs. 11) Then a white robe was given to each of them; and* **it was said to them that they should rest a little while longer, until both the number of their fellow servants and brethren, who would be killed as they were, was completed."**

According to these scriptures, there are going to be many Christians during the Tribulation who are going to be killed for the word of their testimony, just like those who have already died. Again, God has a set number of those who will die during that Tribulation period, then He will bring a finial judgment on the earth. The **sixth seal** is very interesting also, as John was given more details about the Tribulation period. John was given a look at all of the things in the book of Revelation with many details, but all of the things given to him were not necessarily given exactly in order, only to show him that they would all take place.

God has many reasons why He hides secret codes in the scriptures. One of the reasons He hides things is so that His wisdom cannot be understood by human reasoning. He wants His children to search for His hidden secrets, so that they can only understand them in the Spirit, not with their human reasoning. In Chapter 6 of Revelation, God was showing John that something was going to take place during the great Tribulation that was going to be for His divine purpose, to bring glory to Himself. Although He was showing John the revealing of the sixth seal, it was God's purpose to show John what was to take place some time during the great Tribulation. God knew that He could trust John to write everything down in the order that was given to him, not necessarily the order that the event would take place.

In Chapter 6, I found more things about that <u>great day of the Lord's coming.</u> John talks about the sixth seal of God by saying: *Revelation 6:12, "I looked when He opened the* **sixth seal***, and behold,* **there was a great earthquake***; and the* **sun became black** *as* *sackcloth of hair, and* **the moon became like blood**.*"* Please look at what Jesus said in *Matthew 24:29-31 (vs.29)* *"***Immediately after the tribulation of those days** *the* **sun will be darkened**, *and the* **moon will not give its light**; *the* **stars will fall from heaven**, *and* **the powers of the heavens will be shaken**.*"* These two books line up to a T. Can you see it?

Revelation 6:13, "And the stars of heaven fell to the earth, as the fig tree drops its late figs when it is shaken by the mighty wind." This compares to Matthew 24:29 also, almost word for word. This for sure to me is talking a bout the second coming of Christ. How about you? Shall we go on? *Revelation 6:14, "Then the sky receded as a scroll when it is rolled up, and every mountain and island was moved out of its place."* John was being showed when the Second coming of Christ would take place. He saw the same things that Jesus talked about in Matthew 24. Jesus said that right after the great Tribulation those things would take place, then He would come back.

Matthew 24:30, "Then the signs of the Son of Man will appear in heaven, *and then all the tribes of the earth will mourn, and* **they will see the Son of Man coming on the clouds of heaven** *with power and great glory. (vs. 31) And* **He will send His angels with a great sound of a trumpet, and they will**

gather together His elect from the four winds, from one end of heaven to the other."

So this means that Revelation 6:12-17 is going to happen immediately after the first half of the great Tribulation, according to Matthew 24. It is in Revelation 6:17 that John tells us: *"For the great day of His wrath has come, and who is able to stand?"* This means that what John saw happen will not be in the exact order as he recorded it. As I studied the seventh chapter of Revelation, I found some other interesting things about this chapter that caused me to look a little closer at what things were revealed. Everything that was spoken by God or His angels will take place in God's timetable, not according to our knowledge of them. When God showed John the things in the Spirit, He showed John the things that were to take place, either during the great Tribulation or shortly after the great Tribulation.

In Chapter 7, the Lord showed John how an angel was going to seal the 144,000 servants. *Revelation 7:2, "Then I saw another angel ascending from the east, having the* **seal of the living God**. *And he cried with a loud voice to the four angels to whom it was granted to harm the earth and the sea, (vs. 3) saying, 'Do not harm the earth, the sea, or the trees till we have sealed the servants of our God on their foreheads.' (vs.*

4) And I heard the number of those who were sealed. __One hundred and forty-four thousand of all the tribes of the children of Israel were sealed."__

There were 12,000 servants sealed from each of the twelve tribes of Israel, which comes to 144,000. After John saw the six seals that God showed to him, then saw the sealing of the 144,000 of all the tribes of the children of Israel, he then saw something else. He saw a great multitude which no one could number. *Revelation 7:9, "After these things I looked, and behold, a great multitude which no one could number, of all nations, tribes, peoples, and tongues, standing before the throne and before the Lamb, clothed with white robes, with palm branches in their hands."* This proves that there will be many Christians in heaven, not just the 144,000! Now it is time to see some **key words or verses** that can give us new insight to understanding some scriptures. Just overlooking one word could change the meaning of a scripture. *Revelation 7:13, "Then one of the elders answered, saying to me, 'Who are these arrayed in white robes, and where did they come from?'"* The elder asked John a question about this multitude that he saw. It is here that you can find answers about this important question, so look at these scriptures very close, because many people twist these scriptures around to confuse us.

Revelation 7:14, (vs. 14) "And I said to him, 'Sir, you know.' So he said to me, **These are the ones who come out of the great tribulation,** *and washed their robes and made them white in the blood of the Lamb. (vs. 15) Therefore they are before the throne of God, and serve Him day and night in His temple. And He who sits on the throne will dwell among them. (vs. 16) They shall neither hunger any more nor thirst anymore; the sun shall not strike them, nor any heat; (vs. 17) for the Lamb who is in the midst of the throne will shepherd them and lead them to living fountains of water. And God will wipe away every tear from their eyes.'"*

"Who are these arrayed in white robes, and where did they come from?" I too wanted to know who they were, so I had to go to the one who could give the right answers. I asked the Holy Spirit who they were, because some teach that they were the ones who got raptured before the Tribulation. But that is not true, as I will show to you who those people were. *Revelation 7:14, "And I said to him, 'Sir, you know.' So he said to me,* **These are the ones who come out of the great tribulation."'** I was reminded that the word of God is written like no other book that was ever written or will be written. John was given these visions of heaven so that he could write them down. Everything that he

saw was not necessarily in order, but they would be fulfilled in God's timing.

There are two different occasions when God is going to wipe away tears from their eyes. The first time, it will take place at the start of the fourth creation of God, during the 1,000-year reign with Christ. The second time will be in the fifth creation of God, when the new heaven and earth will take place after the great white throne judgment. In verse 14, the elder talking to John said, (vs. 14) "**These are the ones who come out of the great tribulation.**" When he said **come out**, he was saying in the future these ones are going to come out (meaning in the future) of the great Tribulation. In other words, "John, I am showing you these ones now, to show you that after the middle of the great Tribulation, they will be with the Lord forever. They have fought the fight, they did not take the mark of the beast, and they have been washed in the blood of the Lamb." He did not say these are the ones who **came** out of the Tribulation, no, these are the ones who **come** (meaning in the future) out of the Tribulation. Yes, I too did not catch the difference in the wording of those passages. One word can change the meaning of a sentence. Something else caught my attention in these passages also, they are key words that could change the meaning of a sentence also.

May we look at them now? *(vs. 15) "Therefore they are before the throne of God, and* **serve Him day and night in His temple**. *And* **He who sits on the throne will dwell among them."**

Again, the wording in this verse was unclear to me at first, until the Holy Spirit began to explain them unto me. The Elder explained to John the multitude of people's function and what they would be doing in the future after they came out of the great Tribulation. Their task is to serve God before His throne. That part I understood, but in the next part of the verse there are key secret words again that will change the meaning of the verse. John was told that those people were going to: (vs. 15) "**serve Him day and night in His temple.**" I was a little confused, because in God's kingdom, there is no night, so I needed the Holy Spirit to give me understanding in this matter. Could this mean that this must take place on the earth instead of heaven? Also, there is no literal temple in heaven, because the Lord is that temple. "Lord, where is this temple?" When I wrote my book, I was given the address of where that temple will be. The Prophet Ezekiel knows about this hidden temple. In Ezekiel 40-48 is where this earthly temple will be built in the future, just after the great Tribulation and just before the 1,000-year reign with Christ. Now the last part of the verse will make sense: "*And* **He who sits on the throne will dwell among them.**"

In the 1,000-year reign with Christ, He will be their shepherd. Thus, He will lead them (vs.17). I must conclude that the great multitude, which no one could number in *Revelation 7:14-17,* were the ones who made it through the great Tribulation, plus the ones who got Raptured, as well as the ones who rose from the dead. These are the ones John saw before the throne of God. I know that sounds crazy, but it is true. It took me a long time before I was able to see these things through the scriptures I just studied.

I have tried staying away from the book of Revelation, because it is a hard one for me to understand, but God who is mighty wanted me to study its contents by allowing my spirit man to hear what the Spirit is saying to the Church. "Surely Lord," I said, "You have more qualified people to teach on this subject! Nevertheless, at your word I am here to be your servant, so I will write whatever You instruct me to write."

Chapter Fourteen

THE REVEALING OF THE SEVENTH SEAL AND THE SEVEN TRUMPETS

So far in my study time, I saw the judgment of the churches, then the Lamb opened the scroll to reveal unto John what must take place after the judgment of the churches. Next, the seven seals were opened to bring judgment upon the earth, ushering in the great Tribulation period. I must now look at Chapter 8 of Revelation to see what it is about. I noticed that in the fifth seal, it was a cry of the martyrs, who wanted to know how long it would be before the Lord would judge the earth for their blood. In the sixth seal, the Lord showed John something that would take place in the future. Then during the Tribulation, God was going to seal 144,000 servants that were to be His evangelists.

Revelation 8:1, (vs. 1) "When He opened the seventh seal, there was silence in heaven for about half an hour. (vs. 2) And I saw the seven angels who stand before God, and to them were given seven trumpets."

The number seven is used many times in this book, so now it is time to see what these seven trumpets will bring. *(vs. 6) "So the seven angels who had the seven trumpets prepared themselves to sound."*

THE FIRST TRUMPET

Revelation 8:7, "The first angel sounded: And hail and fire followed, mingled with blood, and they were thrown to the earth. And a third of the trees were burned up, and all green grass was burned up."

John was allowed to see the seven angels sound their trumpets. The first four trumpets destroyed many things. The **first trumpet** destroyed a third of the trees and grass on the earth. The **second trumpet,** a third part of the sea became blood, and a third of the living creatures in the sea died. The **third trumpet,** a great star fell on a third of the rivers, causing the water to become bitter and many men died. The **fourth trumpet** caused a third part of the sun, moon, and stars to be darkened.

Revelation 9:1, "Then the **fifth angel sounded**: *And I saw a star fallen from heaven to the earth. To him was given the key to the bottomless pit."* The **fifth trumpet** caused a star to fall upon the earth. To this star was given the key to the bottomless pit. The star was called "him," which meant that this star was a person. This star was an angel of the bottomless pit, who had the name of Abaddon in the Hebrew language and in the Greek he is called Apollyon, which means destruction. Look at: (*vs. 10) "They had tails like scorpions, and there were stings in their tails. Their power was to hurt men five months. (vs. 11) And they had as king over them the angel of the bottomless pit, whose name in Hebrew is Abaddon, but in Greek he has the name Apollyon."* The **fifth trumpet** was also seen by Joel the prophet. He gives us more details in his book concerning the sounding of the trumpet. Again, I am studying these scriptures in the raw form. I am relying on the Holy Spirit's teaching as I study them. I am not trying to interpret the whole book of Revelation, I am just trying to study about the second coming of the Lord and about the day of the Lord. The "Day of the Lord" is used many times in the Bible, both in the Old and New Testaments. When used, it could mean a certain day or a period of time, such as in the great Tribulation.

Joel 1:5, "Awake, you drunkards, and weep; And wail, all you drinkers of wine, Because of the new wine, For it has been cut off from your mouth. (vs. 6) For a nation has come up against My land, Strong, and without number; His teeth are teeth of a lion. (vs. 7) He has laid waste My vine, And ruined My fig tree; He has stripped it bare and thrown it away; Its branches are made white." Yes, Joel goes on and on as to what is going to happen in the great Tribulation period. *(vs. 15)* **"Alas for the day***! For* **the day of the Lord** *is at hand; It shall come as destruction from the Almighty."* The day of the Lord might be a literal day or the whole book of Revelation. It is the day of His judgment upon the earth, the day of the meeting in the air, a day of the judgment of the seven churches. It is the day of His return to the earth to rule and reign for the 1,000 years with His saints. The book of Revelation is the Lord's Day, where He shall reign over the earth forever with His saints.

THE DAY OF THE LORD

Joel 2:1, "Blow the trumpet in Zion, And sound an alarm in My holy mountain! Let all the inhabitants of the land tremble; For **the day of the Lord** *is coming, For it is at hand."*

The blowing of the trumpet is used many times in the Bible, but the trumpet in this verse is a special trumpet, a specific trumpet indeed. It is one of the trumpets that are to be used in the Tribulation period in Revelation for sure, because Joel is a prophet of God, warning God's people that the day of the Lord is at hand when the things he prophesied take place in the great Tribulation of Revelation. Please take note at what things take place in this second chapter of Joel.

Joel 2:2, "A **day of darkness and gloominess**, **A day of clouds and thick darkness**, *Like the morning clouds spread over the mountains. A people come, great and strong, The like of whom has never been; Nor will ever be any such after them, Even for many successive generations."*

Joel is only three chapters long, but it is full of things that pertain to the end times. This is why I am studying them right now. The first part of this second chapter tells about the destruction that is to take place right after the trumpet is blown. Joel describes a special kind of locust that is going to bring destruction upon the earth. *(vs. 3) "A fire devours before them, And behind them a flame burns; The land is like the Garden of Eden before them, And behind them a desolate wilderness; Surly nothing shall escape them, (vs. 4)* **Their**

appearance is like the appearance of horses; *And like swift steeds, so they run.*

This locust had an appearance of horses. They are the same thing that John saw in Revelation 9. They came out of the bottomless pit with a certain king over them: *(vs. 10), "They had tails like scorpions, and there were stings in their tails.* **Their power was to hurt men five months.** *(vs. 11) And they had as* **king over them the angel of the bottomless pit, whose name in Hebrew is Abaddon, but in Greek he has the name Apollyon."** Their purpose was to: **hurt men five months.**

Revelation 9:4, "They were commanded not to harm the grass of the earth, or any green thing, or any tree, but only those men who do not have the seal of God on their foreheads. (vs. 5) And they were not given authority to kill them, but to torment them for five months." Looking back to Joel, these demons, as I call them, were to only hurt men who did not have the seal of God on their foreheads. Kind of like the blood on the doorpost during the Passover, only the seal of God was used during the great Tribulation to protect His 144,000 servants. We must take note of this saying in the word of God: "The day of the Lord."

Joel 2:11, "The Lord gives voice before His army, For His camp is very great; For strong is the One who executes His word. *For* **the day of the Lord** *is great and very terrible; Who can endure it?"*

Again and again "the day of the Lord" shows up in the word of God. Every time this saying appears, it points to the book of Revelation. There have been so many things that have been written about this book of Revelation, so I chose to let the Holy Spirit be my teacher as I studied about the end times. There are many mysteries about this amazing book that I have not read very much, because it was so hard for me to understand.

Joel 2:11, "The Lord gives voice before His army." It is at this time that all of God's children will be with the Lord, in His army, just before Christ comes back to the earth to do battle against the beast and the false prophet. But just before that, God gives one more call for repentance. *(vs. 12) "'Now, therefore,' says the Lord,* **Turn to Me with all your heart, With fasting, with weeping, and with mourning.'"** God loves us so much, even in the great Tribulation the Lord gives His people time to repent of their evil deeds. In the next few verses. It sounds like the Lord is going to refresh the land for a time. Joel is a short book but is packed with prophecy concerning the last days. The coming of the Lord is in two parts, I believe. The first appearance of the Lord will take place just before the last battle takes place, at the end of the first half of the Tribulation. It is then that the first resurrection takes place, when the dead in Christ will be raised from the dead, at which time their bodies will be changed into nonperishable bodies, along with those Christians who are alive at that time whose bodies will also be changed. Both groups will be called up to meet with the Lord in the air. Both the dead in Christ and those who were alive will be given white robes and white horses, so that they will come back to the earth with the Lord to do battle against the beast of the Tribulation period.

But first Joel said that God's Spirit will be poured out one last time before the judgment of the nations. *Joel 2:28, "And it shall come to pass afterward That I will pour out My Spirit on all flesh; Your sons and your daughters shall prophesy; Your old men shall dream dreams, Your young men shall see visions.(vs. 29) And also on My menservants and on My maidservants I will pour out My Spirit in those days."* Peter used these scriptures in the book of Acts, but these scriptures will also be fulfilled in the very last days in the Tribulation. The outpouring of the Holy Spirit takes place from that time in Acts, to just before Christ comes back to the earth the second time. Then the prophet Joel tells us that something else is going to happen just before the Lord comes back to the earth.

Joel 2:30, "And I will show wonders in the heavens and in the earth: Blood and fire and pillars of smoke. (vs. 31) The sun shall be turned into darkness, And the moon into blood, Before the coming of the great and awesome day of the Lord. (vs. 32) And it shall come to pass That whoever calls on the name of the Lord Shall be saved. For in Mount Zion and in Jerusalem there shall be deliverance, As the Lord has said, Among the remnant whom the Lord calls."

It looks like Brother Joel is saying the same thing Jesus said in Matthew 24:29 about the sun and moon. Then in Joel 3:9-17, Joel tells us that some other things are going to take place as well: *(vs. 9) "Proclaim this among the nations:* **'Prepare for war!** *Wake up the mighty men, Let all the men of war draw near,* **Let them come up**.*"'* There is a final call given to the nations to come for this last battle that is to be fought at the end of the Tribulation, in the valley of decision in the valley of Jehoshaphat. *(vs. 14) "Multitudes, multitudes in the valley of decision! For* **the day of the Lord** *is near in the valley of decision."*

There is a key secret in (vs. 9). There is a call to the dead in Christ who were asleep in the graves: **"Wake up the mighty men."** The dead in Christ will arise from the dead to participate in this last battle. These five words are hidden for a reason, so that the blind will not be able to comprehend their meaning. *(vs. 15)* *"The **sun and moon will grow dark**, And the **stars will diminish their brightness**. (vs. 16) The Lord also will roar from Zion, And utter His voice from Jerusalem; The heavens and the earth will shake; But **the Lord will be a shelter for His, people,** And the strength of the children of Israel."* Joel is again saying the same things that Jesus spoke in Matthew 24:29. Everything fell into place as I studied these scriptures about the second coming of the Lord. In the last part of verse 16, Joel tells us how the Lord will protect His people. He will be their shelter, He will call them up to meet Him in the air, so that they can be with Him always.

Joel 3:18, "And **it will come to pass in that day** *That the mountains shall drip with new wine, The hills shall flow with milk, And all the brooks of Judah shall be flooded with water; A fountain shall flow from the house of the Lord. And water the Valley of Acacias."*

Joel is talking about the Fourth Creation of God, which I talk about later in this book. The earth will be renewed for the Fourth time so that all of the rest of prophecy in the Bible can be fulfilled. It is this fourth creation of God that will usher in the 1,000-year reign of Christ with His saints. Now it is time to go back to

Revelation to see what else John saw in his visions of the end times.

THE SIXTH TRUMPET

Revelation 9:13, "Then the sixth angel sounded: And I heard a voice from the four horns of the golden alter which is before God, (vs.14) saying to the sixth angel who had the trumpet, **'Release the four angels** *who are bound at the great river Euphrates.' (vs. 15) So the* **four angels, who had been prepared four the hour and day and month and year, were released to kill a third of mankind."** Here we are, waiting to see what would happen to the earth, as the sixth angel sounded his trumpet. One-third of mankind would be destroyed by these three plagues: *(vs. 18) "by the fire, smoke, and the brimstone which came out of their mouths."*

Chapter Fifteen

THE TWO WITNESSES AND EZEKIEL'S TEMPLE

R evelation 11:1, *"Then I was given a reed like a measuring rod. And the angel stood, saying, 'Rise and* **measure the temple of God,** *the altar, and those who worship there.'"*

I believe that in this place Ezekiel's temple was already built, so that it would be there when Christ returns to the earth at the end of the Tribulation period. It could have been built some time before this verse, because John was just told to measure it, not build it. That means it was already built. John was told about two witnesses to whom God was going to give power: *(vs. 3) "And I will give power to my two witnesses, and they will prophesy one thousand two hundred and sixty days, clothed in sackcloth."* But first many other things were going to happen before that main event was going to take place. The more I studied, the more I became aware that the book of Revelation is very difficult to understand.

Take for instance, the two witnesses. *Zechariah 4:1, "Now the angel who talked with me came back and wakened me, as a man who is wakened out of his sleep. (vs. 2) And he said to me, 'What do you see?' So I said, 'I am looking, and there is a lamp stand of solid gold with a bowl on top of it, and on the stand* **seven lamps** *with seven pipes to the seven lamps. (vs. 3) Two olive trees are by it, one at the right of the bowl, and the other at its left.'"*

Zechariah 4:9, "'The **hands of Zerubbabel** *Have* **laid the foundation of this temple***;* **His hands shall also finish it***. Then you will know That the Lord of host has sent Me to you. (vs. 10) For who has despised the day of small things? For* **these seven rejoice to see***.* **The plumb line in the hand of Zerubbabel.** *They are the* **eyes of the Lord***, Which scan to and fro throughout the whole earth.' ... (vs. 11) Then I answered and said to him, 'What are these* **two olive** trees *at the right of the lamp stand and at its left?' (vs. 12) And I further answered and said to him, 'What are these* **two olive branches** *that drip into receptacles of the two gold pipes from which the golden oil drains?' (vs. 13) Then he answered me and said, 'Do you not* *know what these are?' And I said, 'No, my Lord.' (vs. 14) So he said, 'These are the* **two anointed ones, who stand beside the Lord of the whole earth.'"**

Zerubbabel was a descendant of David (1 Chronicles 3:19). He was leader of the Jewish exiles (Nehemiah 7:6.7; Haggai 2:21-23). He rebuilt the temple (Ezra 3:1-10; Zechariah 4:1-14). These two witnesses are God's special servants, who are going to come to the earth to carry out God's will during the first three-and-a-half years of the Tribulation. They will be given power to do many things. It is during their stay that Ezekiel's temple will be finished. Again, here in these scriptures I was shown secret key words that have secret meaning into the sign of the times during the great Tribulation. First, in *Zechariah 4:2,* **seven lamps.** What are these seven lamps? God uses certain things in scripture to have certain meanings. These seven lamps represent "*... the* **eyes of the Lord***, Which scan to and fro throughout the whole earth."* (vs. 10). As we can see, these lamps are important because they go all over the earth so that God can see what is hap-pening. We will never know all of God's secrets, but He will reveal them to whoever He chooses. I always thought about how God could see everywhere at the same time. The Bible tells us that God has seven Spirits. These lamps could also be the seven Spirits.

In the book of Revelation, there are seven Spirits of God mentioned that are over the seven churches.

THE MYSTERY OF THE SEVENTH TRUMPET OF GOD

Again I am reminded that the **Bible is written in numbers, parables, and codes,** therefore the order of the writings of the scriptures can only be solved by the Holy Spirit, who was sent to us as our teacher. God wants us to rely on Him for everything. He expects us to seek Him through His word, for the hidden treasures that are written within His word. I know that there are only two main resurrections talked about in the New Testament, which are the main events other than our Lord Jesus Christ's resurrection. He is the firstborn from the dead so that He could be first in all things. So with that being said, I had some more questions that I needed answered from the Holy Spirit of God. My first question to the Holy Spirit was when I read Revelation 11:11-14: "When the Lord called the two witnesses up to heaven, was that a resurrection also?" He told me to back up and read from verse seven. So I did, then it became clearer about what happened. What did I see? I saw that the beast from the bottomless pit made war on them and killed them, but not until they finished their testimony.

They lay on the streets for three-and-a-half days. They were not buried. Now in (vs. 11), *"Now after the three-and-a-half days the breath of life from God entered them, and they stood on their feet, and great fear fell on those who saw them."* They were killed, but they were not buried. They did not need to be resurrected, because they came from heaven in the first place. They just needed the breath of God to bring them back to life. They were here for the purpose of witnessing to the people. They were sent in human form, so when they were finished with their assignment from God, He allowed their bodies to be killed. *Revelation 11:12, "And they heard a loud voice from heaven saying to them, 'Come up here.' And* **they ascended to heaven in a cloud**, *and their enemies saw them."*

I feel excitement in the air! The seventh trumpet just sounded, the two witnesses just came back to life after being dead for three-and-a-half days, then there was a call from heaven for them to come up to heaven. Hold on! More things are about to take place. If we could only see into the future the way the prophets saw things, then our eyes would behold the secrets of God's plan, or maybe just a little bit of them. Jonah was in the belly of the whale for three days, Jesus was in the grave for three days, now these two witnesses were dead for only three days. Yes! I believe supernatural things are taking place, as the Holy Spirit begins to reveal **secret codes** in this study. "**They ascended to heaven in a cloud.**" Are these two witnesses the only ones being called up to heaven at this time?

Brother John saw things that were to take place when the seventh trumpet was to be sounded. There was a shift in power taking place at this time also in the heavenly realm, where the kingdoms of the world were being taken over by the creator of the universe. Now look at the next verse. *Revelation 11:13, "In that* **same hour** *there was a* **great earthquake,** *and a tenth of the city fell. In the earth-quake* **seven thousand people were killed,** *and the rest were afraid and gave glory to the God of heaven."* Again there are key secrets in these verses that were revealed unto me. "*In that same hour*" shows that there are other things to take place in that same hour; "*there was a great earthquake,*" then, "*a tenth of the city fell.*" There is something about the phrase, "*In that* **same hour.**" What hour is John talking about here? The same hour that the two witnesses were called up to heaven, there was an earthquake that killed 7,000 people. Also in that same hour the seventh trumpet sounded. This particular hour is a prophetic hour of events, not an ordinary hour of sixty minutes as some think.

Chapter Sixteen

THE SEVENTH TRUMPET AND THE KINGDOM IS PROCLAIMED

Revelation 11:15, *"Then the seventh angel sounded: And there were loud voices in heaven, saying,* <u>**The kingdoms of this world have become the kingdoms of our Lord and of His Christ, and He shall reign forever and ever!"***</u>

In my quest to find scripture on the second coming of Christ, I came across this verse. So as I was looking at it, I was a little confused about the timing of the **Seventh trumpet** being sounded. I asked the Holy Spirit to reveal its meaning to me so that I could know the truth. Many things happen during the sounding of the **Seventh trumpet**. A proclamation was just made here in (vs. 15), proclaiming that the kingdoms of the world have already become the kingdoms of our Lord. The sounding of the **Seventh trumpet** ushered in that revelation to John. This **Seventh trumpet** established an atmosphere in the supernatural realm for the transfer of ownership of those kingdoms to take place. It was established as being done already in heaven, because in God's kingdom God sees things before they actually take place. The things of God are established in the heavenly realm way before they happen on earth, even before the earth was formed in the beginning of time.

So when John received that revelation, he heard the sounding of the **Seventh trumpet** in the heavenly realm, which means that it was imminent, that it was going to happen on the earth soon. But first many other things were going to happen before that main event would take place. The two witnesses' work was finished, the first three-and-a-half years of the great Tribulation were now over. Now they were called up to heaven. The sounding of the **Seventh trumpet** set in motion a change in the heavenly realm, as well as a change in the earthly realm.

God's judgment of His wrath was about to be poured over the earth. There is a great mystery about to be revealed in the last half of this great Tribulation period. Remember, there are **key secrets** in the word of God that need to be unlocked, so that we can know what

John is talking about. Revelation 11:15-19 is packed with information on what is about to happen in the chapters before us. The **Seventh trumpet** of God is a profound example into understanding some of the mysteries of God's word. The **Seventh trumpet**, when sounded, brought in an atmosphere of change in the kingdom of the earth as well as in the kingdom of heaven. Look at verse 17 with me: *vs. 17, "...saying: 'We give You thanks, O Lord God Almighty, The* **One who is and who was and who is to come, Because You have taken Your great power and reigned.'"** From this moment on, God took complete power to reign over everything. Satan, lost his power, or what little power he had, from this moment on. Now in the next verse, the sounding of that seventh trumpet ushered in God's wrath and judgment: *vs. 18, "The* **nations were angry,** *and* **Your wrath has come,** *And the* **time of the dead, that they should be judged,** *And that* **You should reward Your servants the prophets and the saints,** *And* **those who fear Your name, small and great,** *And* **should destroy those who destroy the earth."**

There are seven things that are to take place according to John, mentioned in this verse. They will all take place after the sounding of the seventh trumpet of God. I am not going to try to interpret all of them for you, I just want you to be aware that God works in signs, as well as numbers in His word, like these seven things mentioned right here. I now want to move on to the next chapter to see what is coming next.

I have spent some time looking at this chapter so that I may be able to understand what John saw in Chapter Twelve. John saw three things in the first six verses of this chapter. The first seven words recorded here in this chapter are very important. *12:1, "Now a great sign appeared in heaven."* A lot of different people in the Bible always asked for a sign because of their unbelief. If they would have truly believed in God's word, they would not need a sign. By the way, I include myself when I say that. Everyone needs a sign so that their faith might be built up. In other words, show me something to prove what you are saying is true.

First, John saw a strange woman: *(vs. 1), "... a woman clothed with the sun, with the moon under her feet, and on her head a garland of twelve stars."* This to me was a strange description of a woman, but then I was reminded that this description of the woman here was for a sign, not an actual woman. This woman represented someone of great character, so whose character did this woman represent? The number Twelve is used many times in the Bible: Twelve tribes of Israel, Twelve disciples, Twelve stars.

The woman was clothed with the sun, showing that she was clothed with righteousness, the moon was under her feet, showing that she was above the earth, her thoughts were above the earth, and they were on heavenly things. It all started in Geneses with Eve: *Genesis 3:15, "And I will put enmity between you and the woman, and between your seed and her Seed; He shall bruise your head, and you shall bruise His heel."* Yes, it all started back in Genesis 3:15, so now John was being showed a history lesson through the signs that he saw in chapter twelve. There were three characters in Genesis: the woman, the seed, and of course, Satan.

Eve was the mother of all mankind. She had the seed or the child, which was the Church, within herself. Jesus came through that lineage, therefore when He was born into this world, Satan tried to destroy Him. After His resurrection, He was caught up to God. From that time on, Satan or the dragon waged war on the woman's seed or offspring. In (vs. 6), John is shown what happens in the last half of the great Tribulation period.

Now in (vs. 7), something happens to Satan and his kingdom. An all-out war began in heaven that was exciting. *Revelation 12:7, (vs. 7) "And war broke out in heaven: Michael and his angels fought with the dragon; and the* **dragon** *and* **his angels fought,** *(vs.8) but* **they did not prevail, nor was a place found for them in heaven any** *longer."* Here is another example of how God works behind the scenes. God already takes care of things in the heavenly realm before they happen in the earthly realm. The dragon and Satan are already defeated in the heavenly realm before they are defeated on the earthly realm later on. There is a shift in power from this time on!

Revelation 12:10, "Then I heard a loud voice saying in heaven, 'Now **salvation** *and* **strength,** *and the* **kingdom of our God,** *and* **the power of His Christ have come,** *for* **the accuser of our brethren, who accused them before our God day and night, has been cast down.'"**

Finally Satan is kicked out of heaven! All he did was to accuse God's children of everything, day and night, but God put a stop to his accusations once and for all. John said that now salvation and strength has come, Satan has been cast down to the earth, therefore the earth should be aware that he will be coming to the earth with a bad attitude. Up to this time in my study, I did not see any scripture that specifically stated that the Rapture of the Church was going to take place before the great Tribulation. In this twelfth chapter of Revelation, John talks about three individuals: the woman, the child, and the dragon. I talked about these three individuals already, but I did want to mention that John is getting ready to talk about the woman in the next few verses again. Now that the dragon has been cast to the earth, he is going to finish persecuting the seed or offspring of the woman, which means that the Rapture has not occurred as of yet.

Revelation 12:13, "Now when the dragon saw that he had been cast to the earth, he persecuted the woman who gave birth to the male Child."

I am now going to move ahead to chapter of Revelation 14, because I am not here to interpret the whole book of Revelation. That is not my purpose. I am seeking to find out when the Rapture is to take place. This brings me to the fourteenth chapter of Revelation. I was shown some very interesting things in this chapter, so I thought that I would show them to you at this time. It is in this chapter that John saw two things that were interesting: first he saw a Lamb standing on Mount Zion; then he saw with the Lamb the 144,000. These 144,000 servants, who **were sealed during the Tribulation**, are not talked about much during the Tribulation. Yet here they are standing on Mount Zion with the Lamb. Which Mount Zion was this? The one on the earth or the one in heaven?

I was a little confused myself, so I was led to look a little bit closer at the next few verses. John did not say if they were killed, then resurrected to get there, or if they were taken alive. So now, let us take a close look at what John saw.

Revelation 14:1, "Then I looked, and behold, a Lamb standing on Mount Zion, and with Him one hundred and forty-four thousand, having His Father's name written on their foreheads."

There is a heavenly Mount Zion that is recorded in: *Hebrews 12:18-24.* The writer of Hebrews knew that there was a heavenly Mount Zion as well. In verses 18-21, he explains which mountain they have not come to, because in verses 22-24 he explains the heavenly Mount Zion is the one they have come to. *12:18, "For you have not come to the mountain that may be touched and that burned with fire."* Then in (vs. 22), *"But you have come to Mount Zion and to the city of the living God."* So right here is proof that there are two Mount Zion's. Here is another time that the earthly Mount Zion is mentioned in the Bible: *Zechariah 14:3, (vs. 3) "Then the Lord will go forth and fight those nations, As* **He fights in the day of battle**. *(vs.4) and* **in that day His feet will stand on the Mount of Olives**, *Which faces Jerusalem on the east. And the Mount of Olives shall be split in two,* *from east to west, making a very large valley; half of the mountain shall move toward the north and half of it toward the south."*

So after I was reading these scriptures, I need to go back to Revelation 14, so that I can show you which Mount Zion John is talking about: the one on earth or the one in heaven. In the next few verses lie some secret key verses that will give us understanding into some of the mysteries of the creations of God.

14:2, "And I heard a voice from heaven, like the voice of many waters, and like the voice of loud thunder. And I heard the sound of harpists playing their harps. (vs. 3) They sang as it were a new song before the throne, before the four living creatures, and the elders; and **no one could learn that song except the hundred and forty-four thousand who were redeemed from the earth."** Here is proof that the 144,000 were in heaven at this time. A past tense is used that states: **"who were redeemed from the earth,"** which means it already happened. First John saw the Lamb and the 144,000 standing on Mount Zion, then he heard a voice from heaven. At the same time, he heard music and singing from the 144,000 singing a new song to which only they knew the words. Then in, (vs. 4, 5), he was told who these 144,000 were: *(vs. 4), "These are* **the ones who were not**

defiled with woman, *for they are virgins. These are the* **ones who follow the Lamb** *wherever He goes. These* **were redeemed from among men, being first fruits to God and to the Lamb. (***Vs. 5) And in their mouth was found no deceit, for they are without fault before the throne of God."* Key verse: *"These* **were redeemed from among men, being first fruits to God and to the Lamb."**

This transformation could have already taken place in Revelation 12:5. The Lord wanted these 144,000 to be the first ones caught up to meet Him in the clouds. In Chapter 14 they are in heaven, I believe, and they are not mentioned after Chapter 14. But hold on; there are more things about to take place in that same moment of time. This certain day of the Lord is a big day indeed, as I am about to reveal to you in just a moment. The **key** to understanding scriptures is in seeking the treasure that lies within them. To find the truth that is in the word of God, one must meditate day and night on the things that you are seeking after. The holy scriptures are not just mere words, not at all. The words of God are life and wisdom.

The sounding of the **Seventh trumpet** ushered in many things also. More than one thing is going to happen. May we go back to the eleventh chapter of Revelation for a refreshing look at this seventh trumpet? Each of the Seven Trumpets had a different task to perform, and the task of each trumpet took so many days to accomplish. How many days, I am not sure, but again this is not my purpose to figure these things out. I am going through this study for one purpose: to find out when the Rapture is to take place.

Now the **Seventh trumpet** is a very interesting trumpet indeed. The length of time is important, but how many days it lasted I am not sure. Just before the Seventh trumpet sounded, something happened. The two witnesses, after being dead for three-and-a-half days, came back to life. Then they were called to come up to heaven. It is right after this that the Seventh trumpet sounded. God had a plan as to why these two witnesses were to be the first ones called up to heaven during the great Tribulation. I cannot tell you that because the writer of this book said not to add anything to it or take anything out, so I needed to draw a line so that I do not cross over.

Revelation 11:15, "Then the seventh angel sounded: And there were loud voices in heaven, saying, **The kingdoms of this world have become the kingdoms of our Lord and of His Christ, and He shall reign forever and ever!'"**

Here is the purpose or objective of the Seventh trumpet: the sounding of this seventh trumpet was to set into motion a chain of events that would cause these things to take place. I talked about this earlier in this book. The sounding of the seventh trumpet lasted from Revelation 11:15 to chapter 15. So now in the fourteenth chapter, everything listed in this chapter is still under the sounding of the seventh trumpet of God.

Chapter Seventeen

THE PROCLAMATION OF THREE ANGELS

I often wondered how John was able to handle all of these revelations. I suppose that it came about by him being in the Spirit. If John had been in the flesh, he might have had a heart attack or even could have died. I am experiencing excitement myself as these things are being revealed to me. I can almost find myself beside myself. For me to understand these things, I had to disregard some of my old teaching to make room for the new. I had to be in the Spirit to understand these deep teachings. I found myself shaking my head in amazement because of the things that the Spirit taught me.

*Revelation 14:6, "Then I saw **another angel flying in the midst of heaven**, having the **everlasting gospel** to preach to those who dwell on the earth-to* every nation, tribe, tongue, and people- (vs. 7) saying with a loud voice, 'Fear God and give glory to Him, for **the hour of His judgment has come;** and worship Him who made heaven and earth, the sea and springs of water.'"

That means that this far into the Tribulation, there will be time for people to get their life right with the Lord, or else why still preach to those people? This angel John saw had the task of preaching the "**everlasting gospel**" throughout the whole earth, telling them to fear God for "**the hour of His judgment has come.**" He was talking about the **Bowl Judgments** that would take place very shortly. God is merciful because He gives people time to turn from their wicked ways, even this far into the great Tribulation period. Now the second of the three angels that John saw had a different task: (Rev.14:8), "And another angel followed, saying, 'Babylon is fallen, is fallen, that great city, because she has made all nations drink of the wine of the wrath of her fornication.'"

Here again, John was shown by this angel what was going to happen in the future because the fall of Babylon did not take place until chapter 18 of this book. The angel was just making this proclamation in the heavenly realm, in an atmosphere of the supernatural realm as fact, that it will take place shortly. The **key** to understanding this verse is in the proclamation. By speaking it out in faith, that thing will take place, for the power of the tongue comes from speaking it as already done, although it has not yet manifested in the natural. *Revelation 14:9, (vs. 9) "Then a third angel followed them, saying with a loud voice, 'If anyone worships the beast and his image, and receives his mark on his forehead or on his hand, (vs.10) he himself shall drink of the wine of the wrath of God, which is poured out full strength into the cup of His indignation. He shall be tormented with fire and brimstone in the presence of the holy angels and in the presence of the Lamb.'"*

Revelation 14:13, "Then I heard a voice from heaven saying to me, 'Write: **"Blessed are the dead who die in the Lord from now on.**" *'Yes,' says the Spirit, 'that they may rest from their labors, and their works follow them.'"*

The important message in this verse is for those who are left behind after the Rapture that will take place in the next three verses. There are key secrets in these verses that helped me to understand what was going on. The key words are: (vs. 14) **"a white cloud**." There was something special about this cloud, so please read it now.

REAPING OF THE EARTH'S HARVEST

*Revelation 14:14, "Then I looked, and behold, **a white cloud**, and **on the cloud sat One like the Son of Man**, having on His head a golden crown, and **in His hand a sharp sickle.**"*

What John saw was important because he always says "behold," which means look at it intently, directing your attention to it with everything you have. John saw a **white cloud** with the Lord sitting on it. John knew that this was the same cloud that Matthew saw with Christ coming back in the clouds, to do His reaping of the earth's harvest. This is the event that is going to happen just before the seven bowl judgments. God is calling all of His children up to meet with Him in the clouds. This is part one of the return of Christ. When Christ comes this time, every eye will see Him as the heavens open up. He is only coming after His elect, therefore, everyone who is born again, both the dead in Christ and those who are alive on the earth at this Second coming of the Lord. Just a reminder, the next time Christ returns to the earth, He is coming back with all the saints to do battle with the beast. This takes place in Revelation 19.

Revelation 14:15, "And another angel came out of the temple, crying with a loud voice to Him who sat on the cloud, '**Thrust in Your sickle and reap, for the time has come for You to reap, for the harvest of the earth is ripe.**' *(vs. 16) So He who sat on the cloud thrust in His sickle on the earth, and* **the earth was reaped**." God has not appointed His children for wrath. This is why I believe that He has chosen this time in the Tribulation to call His children to come be with Him from this time forward. What is the Rapture of the Church? Is this the time in Revelation it is going to happen? Please look at Matthew with me to compare these scriptures.

Here is where Mathew and John connect regarding the rapture. Can you see the connection? *Matthew 24:29-31, (vs.29)* "**Immediately after the tribulation of those days** *the sun will be darkened, and the moon will not give its light; the stars will fall from heaven, and the powers of the heavens will be shaken.* **(vs. 30) Then the signs of the Son of Man will appear in heaven,** *and then all the tribes of the earth will mourn,* *and* **they will see the Son of Man coming on the clouds of heaven** *with power and great glory. (vs. 31) And* **He will send His angels with a great sound of a trumpet, and they will gather together His elect from the four winds, from one end of heaven to the other.**"

{There is the reaping of the earth's harvest first, then the reaping of the grapes of wrath. It is at this time God will separate the good from the bad. Blessed be our God, who is rich in mercy, who has delivered us from the wrath that was to come from the seven angels, who had the last seven bowls of God's wrath.}

First, I will talk about the first harvest of the earth. Both Matthew and John saw the first harvest coming in these scriptures. There is going to be a gathering of God's elect according to Matthew, because he goes into great detail in the verses that follow the ones I just mentioned. But first, let me show you what these verses have in common. Matthew said: *(vs. 29)* "**Immediately after the tribulation of those days,**" certain things were going to happen. To understand this verse, I must explain what days Matthew was talking about. The great Tribulation of Revelation is divided by many days. The first three-and-a-half years of the first part of the great Tribulation are what Matthew was talking about. I say that because there are two times that Christ is going to come back. So immediately after the first half of the Tribulation, Jesus is going to gather His elect from all parts of the world. This gathering will take place in the clouds -- which, by the way is what we call the Rapture. (Vs. 30), "**they will see the Son of Man coming on the clouds**

of heaven." Matthew does not say that Christ will touch the earth at this time, because this time He is coming for His elect group, which is all believers that have been born again. (Vs. 31), "**they will gather together His elect from the four winds, from one end of heaven to the other.**" This all happens at the sounding of the seventh trumpet.

Now look at what John saw: *Revelation 14:14, (vs.14) "Then I looked, and behold,* **a white cloud**, *and* **on the cloud sat One like the Son of Man,** *having on His head a golden crown, and* **in His hand a sharp sickle.** *(vs. 15) And another angel came out of the temple, crying with a loud voice to Him who sat on the cloud, 'Thrust in Your sickle and reap, for the time has come for You to reap, for the harvest of the earth is ripe.' (vs. 16) So He who sat on the cloud thrust in His sickle on the earth, and the earth was reaped."* Yes! It is harvest time for the saints of God.

Matthew did continue on the subject of the Rapture of the Church in chapters 24 and 25. All of the Parables that followed Matthew 24:29-31 give us clues about the second coming of our Lord in that meeting in the clouds. Remember, there are two comings of the Lord recorded in the scriptures. This one in Matthew is the first one. I explain about the second one later on, which happens when Christ comes back to the earth, riding on a horse with all of the saints who were Raptured during Christ's appearance on the clouds. Now from this time forward the wrath of God's judgment will be poured out. The second part of His reaping will take place in the next few verses.

REAPING THE GRAPES OF WRATH

Revelation 14:17, (vs. 17) "Then another angel came out of the temple which is in heaven, he also having a sharp sickle. (vs. 18) Then another angel came out from the altar, who had power over fire, and he cried with a loud cry to him who had the sharp sickle, saying, 'Thrust in your sharp sickle and gather the cluster of the vine of the earth, for her grapes are fully ripe.'"

Now that the reaping of the earth was complete, by the catching away of the saints and every born again believer, God was about to pour out His wrath upon those who were left behind. This second reaping of God's wrath will be performed during the last battle at the end of the great Tribulation.

Chapter Eighteen

THE SEVEN BOWLS OF GOD'S WRATH

Revelation 16:1, *"Then I heard a loud voice from the temple saying to the seven angels, 'Go and pour out the bowls of the wrath of God on the earth.'"* The wrath of God is about to be poured out on the earth to everyone who had the mark of the beast. This means that there are still those who did not take the mark of the beast at this time, so they were not saved as of yet or they would have been taken up with the rest of the saints. These bowls of the wrath of God come with plagues similar to the ones that Israel had when they were in Egypt, before they crossed through the Red Sea. God waited all of these years to pour out His wrath on ungodly men. So now at His appointed time, He sent His angels to pour out the seven bowls

of wrath. Up till now He gave the people time to repent, but they refused.

The **first bowl**: *Revelation 16:2, "So the first went and poured out his bowl upon the earth, and a foul and loathsome sore came upon the men who had the mark of the beast and those who worshiped his image."* These terrible sores came upon only the ones who had the mark of the beast or who worshiped its image. The key to this verse is who received these terrible sores.

The **second bowl**: *(vs. 3) "Then the second angel poured out his bowl on the sea, and it became blood as of a dead man; and every living creature in the sea died."* The sea became blood just like God did to the Egyptians.

The **third bowl**: *(vs. 4) "Then the third angel poured out his bowl on the rivers and springs of water, and they became blood."* So that means every water supply has now become blood. How long can man survive with no water supply? Why God did these things is revealed in the next three verses. The answer is in (vs. 6), *"For they have shed the blood of saints and prophets, And You have given them blood to drink. For it is their just due."* They got what they deserved as one of their punishments.

The **fourth bowl**: *(vs. 8)* *"Then the fourth angel poured out his bowl on the sun, and power was given to him to scorch men with fire. (vs. 9) And men were scorched with great heat, and they blasphemed the name of God who has power over the plagues; and they did not repent and give Him glory."* The key to this verse is in the very last few words: *"they did not repent and give Him glory."* If the people would have repented and given God the glory He deserved, they would not have been tormented in that fashion.

The **fifth bowl**: *(vs. 10)* *"Then the fifth angel poured out his bowl on the throne of the beast, and his kingdom became full of darkness; (vs. 11) They blasphemed the God of heaven because of their pains and sores, and did not repent of their deeds."* Again they did not repent, so God poured out yet another plague, which was darkness. God's love is still available even in His judgments upon the earth, because each time God allowed the people to repent.

The **sixth bowl**: *(vs. 12)* *"Then the sixth angel poured out his bowl on the great river Euphrates, and its water was dried up, so that the way of the kings from the east might be prepared."* The sixth bowl here is a bowl of wrath that is used for a preparation for the last battle of the Tribulation period, when Christ will come back to the earth to defeat the beast and to bind up Satan for 1,000 years. The river must be dried up so that all of the armies from all the nations can cross over that river, because they will be coming on horses.

I believe that God is going to launch His own cyber attack on the earth. There are more clues about this sixth bowl that involve three evil demon spirits who go out to all the kings of the earth, so they can come for that great battle of all times. I believe that this sixth bowl will happen just before the return of Christ to the earth because they will all have to be there when that happens. Now the seventh bowl will not happen until Christ is ready to come back to the earth, because in chapter 17 and 18 many things must take place first. Then in chapter 19 Christ comes back to the earth.

The **seventh bowl**: (*vs. 17*) *"Then the seventh angel poured out his bowl into the air, and a loud voice came out of the temple of heaven, from the throne, saying, 'It is done!'* This verse refers to the point in time when Christ comes to the earth and defeats the beast. The Lord will reign with His saints for 1,000 years. This is why when John saw the things he saw, they were not in perfect order, only the fact that they will take place. The seventh bowl will be God's final wrath, which will take place just before He returns to the earth. Its primary purpose is for the Mystery, Babylon that will take place in the next two chapters. Verses 17-21 reveal what God is about to do just before the Lord comes back to the earth. (Vs. 17): the angel makes a proclamation to John by saying, *"It is done!"* The revelation comes from heaven that God's judgment of His wrath is done when the bowl is poured out on the earth. It is seem as a fact because the atmosphere in the heavenly realm already sees the result before it actually takes place. God sees it already done. Now in the next four verses, I will show you some other things that will take place from this seventh bowl of the wrath of God.

Revelation 16:18, "And there were noises and thundering and lightning's; and there was a great earthquake, **such a mighty and great earthquake** *as had not occurred since men were on the earth."*

Revelation 16: look at (vs. 19) *"Now the great city was divided into three parts, and the cities of the nations fell. And great Babylon was remembered before God, to give her the cup of the wine of the fierceness of His wrath."* The earthquake was so strong that Babylon was divided into three parts, plus, whole cities fell. The great earthquake also caused every island to disappear. Not only that, but every mountain was not found either. Then great hailstones fell from heaven on men. Many things have been written about this great book of Revelation. Again, I am not here to teach on this great book, but I am looking in this great book for answers about the coming of our Lord.

The fall of Babylon the Great is the subject in chapter 18. Babylon will fall just before the Lord returns to the earth to defeat the beast, then He will set up His kingdom on the earth. Let me back up to: *Revelation 17:15, "Then he said to me, 'The waters which you saw, where the harlot sits, are peoples, multitudes, nations, and tongues. (vs. 16) And the ten horns which you saw on the beast, these will hate the harlot, make her desolate and naked, eat her flesh and burn her with fire. (vs. 17)* **For God has put it into their hearts to fulfill His purpose, to be of one mind, and to give their kingdom to the beast**, *until the words of God are fulfilled. (vs. 18) And the woman whom you saw is that great city which reigns over the kings of the earth.'"*

I find it amazing how God can make His enemies do things to fulfill His purpose. He put it in their hearts to do the things He wanted done. God wanted the beast to take over the earth for this one last time, until he was released after the 1,000-year reign, because He was ready now to send His Son back to the earth to defeat the beast, then to cast Satan into the bottomless pit for 1,000 years. I can hardly wait. How about you? Here again in Chapter 18, John saw another angel coming down from heaven to tell John why that great city of Babylon fell. *Revelation 18:7, "In the measure that she glorified herself and lived luxuriously, in the same measure give her torment and sorrow; for she says in her heart, 'I sit as queen, and I am no widow, and will not see sorrow.' (vs. 8)* **Therefore her plagues will come in one day -- death and morning and famine. And she will be utterly burned with fire, for strong is the Lord God who judges her."**

God hates the spirit of pride; "**her plagues will come in one day -- death."** Here is another saying about one day judgments. Babylon the great city will be no more because of God's judgment on her. She was called the Mystery Babylon. I believe that this mystery Babylon could be the United States of America. I know that most Bible teachers will not agree with that, but that is okay, this is just a thought that I had. The United States is the melting pot of all of the languages of the world. She fits the descriptions of the mystery Babylon in many areas. It is not my purpose right now to teach on this subject, so I will move on to find the answers about the second coming of Christ.

Revelation 18:21, "Then a mighty angel took up a stone like a great millstone and threw it into the sea, saying, 'Thus with violence the great city Babylon shall be thrown down, and shall not be found anymore.'" We are now in the fourth quarter of the biggest event, which will bring the end of the Third Creation of God and bring us into the Fourth Creation of God. Excitement filled the air when that great city of Babylon fell and was found no more. John was about to be shown why everyone in heaven was so excited! *Revelation 19:1, "After these things I heard a loud voice of a great multitude in heaven, saying, 'Alleluia! Salvation and glory and honor and power belong to the Lord our God! (vs. 2) For true and righteous are His judgments, because He has judged the great harlot who corrupted the earth with her fornication; and He has avenged on her the blood of His servants shed by her.'"* This will now take us to the second coming of Christ on the white horse. Everything began to make more sense now as I took a closer look at the word of God. May God receive all the glory, because this book belongs to Him.

Chapter Nineteen

CHRIST ON A WHITE HORSE

Here Is John's Vision Of That Last Battle Of The Tribulation

The Holy Spirit said to me, "Look! Over there, is that a white horse coming from the sky?" The brightness of the Lord Jesus almost blinded me, because He was not alone. The armies of heaven were coming with Him.

Revelation 19:11- 16, (vs. 11) "Now I saw heaven opened, and behold, a white horse. And He who sat on him was called Faithful and True, and in righteousness He judges and makes war. (vs. 12) His eyes were like a flame of fire, and on His head were many crowns. He had a name written that no one knew except himself. (vs.

13) He was clothed with a robe dipped in blood, and His name is called The Word of God. (vs. 14) And the armies in heaven, clothed in fine linen, white and clean, followed Him on white horses. (vs. 15) Now out of His mouth goes a sharp sword, that with it He should strike the nations. And **He Himself will rule them with a rod of iron***. He Himself treads the winepress of the fierceness and wrath of Almighty God. (vs. 16) And He has on His robe and on His thigh a name written:* **KING OF KINGS AND LORD OF LORDS."**

One of the most interesting battles was now going to take place right before my eyes. The Lord God and Jesus Christ will go to battle the old Serpent (Satan), so that He can bind up Satan for a period of 1,000 years. What a spectacular sight it was to see the whole armies of God riding on white horses, with the King of Kings leading them into this great battle. **{Again, each of us who are going on this journey must use our imagination in the spirit, to be able to visualize what it would look like, as if we were actually able to see it in person. In the spirit I was able to see these things. You too can see them if you look through your spiritual eyes.}**

I could hardly wait to see Satan defeated so that the earth could be returned to the condition it was meant to be in, before the fall of man. Every place Satan had been in, there was trouble. He has messed up every creation that God has made, in some way. Now his time had come to be locked up for 1,000 years. To get the whole picture of this battle in comparison to Ezekiel's battle, we must look at both of these books.

The **key factor** is the **feast of the birds and the beast** of the field. *Revelation 19:17-21, (vs. 17) "Then I saw an angel standing in the sun; and he cried with a loud voice, <u>saying to all the **birds** that fly in the midst of heaven, 'Come and gather together for the **supper of the great God**,</u> (vs. 18) that you may eat the flesh of kings, the flesh of captains, the flesh of mighty men, the flesh of horses and of those who sit on them, and the flesh of all people, free and slave, both small and great.' (vs. 19) And I **saw the beast**, the kings of the earth, and their armies, gathered together to make war against Him who sat on the horse and against His army. (vs. 20) Then **the beast was captured**, and with him the <u>false prophet</u> who worked signs in his presence, by which he deceived those who received the mark of the beast and those who worshiped his image.* **These two were cast alive into the lake of fire burning with brimstone.** *(vs. 21.) And the rest* *were killed with the sword which proceeded from the mouth of Him who sat on the horse. **And all the birds were filled with their flesh.**"*

Can you see it yet? Look at **Ezekiel 39:4, "'You shall fall upon the mountains of Israel, you and your troops and the peoples who are with you; I will give you to birds of prey of every sort and to the beast of the field to be devoured. (vs. 5) You shall fall on the open field; for I have spoken,' says the Lord God."** Both John and Ezekiel are talking about the same battle. They both received their visions from God, even though they were in different durations of time, separated by many years. The "day" that the Lord talked about so much in the Old Testament came to pass in Revelation 19:*11-16*. Many things will happen that day. The Lord is going to clean house on this earth, including taking care of Satan by locking him up for 1,000 years.

The next thing I need to do is to show you what happened after this great battle. But first look at the things that are to happen that "day": **(Ezekiel 38:19, "Surely in that day there shall be a great earthquake in the land of Israel, (vs. 20) so that the fish of the sea, the birds of the heavens, the beast of the field, all creeping things that creep on the earth, and all men who are on the face of the earth shall**

shake at My presence. The mountains shall be thrown down, the steep places shall fall, and every wall shall fall to the ground." Also that is when the marriage of the Lamb and the Church: **Revelation 19:7, 8, (vs. 7) "Let us be glad and rejoice and give Him glory, for the marriage of the Lamb has come, and His wife has made herself ready."** Then Christ gathers His armies to do battle, so that He can prepare the marriage supper for His bride. The beast and the false prophet were "...*cast alive into the lake of fire burning with brimstone.*" Then Satan is locked up for 1,000 years. What a day that will be!

THE BURIAL OF GOG

Ezekiel 39:12, 13, (vs. 12) "For seven months the house of Israel will be burying them, in order to cleanse the land. (vs. 13) Indeed all the people of the land will be burying, and they will gain renown for it on the day that I am glorified,' says the Lord God." That was for sure a long time for Israel to be burying all of the dead bodies. They even sent search parties out after the seven months, to make sure all of the dead bodies were buried. According to Ezekiel 39, 40 is when Israel is restored in the fourth creation. Right after this great battle, the beast and the false prophet were cast alive into the lake of fire, this was a sight to behold! For they had done many bad things during the Tribulation period. This battle was truly a bloody one indeed. I am sure glad that I was in my time capsule so that I was not killed in that battle. But the greatest thing that happened in this was that the serpent, that old devil (Satan), would be bound up for 1,000 years.

Look over there with me! There is an angel. He is not an ordinary angel, because He had a key, a special key for sure. The only one I know who has a key like that one is Jesus Christ. He is the only one who is strong enough to bind the devil, because all power in heaven and the earth belongs to the Lord Jesus Christ.

Revelation 20:1-3, **"Then I saw an angel coming down from heaven, having <u>the key to the bottomless pit and a great chain in his hand.</u>** *(vs. 2)* **He laid hold of the dragon, that serpent of old, who is the Devil and Satan, and bound him for a thousand years; (vs. 3) And cast him into the bottomless pit, and shut him up, and set a seal on him, so that he should not <u>deceive the</u>** <u>*nations no more till the thousand years were finished. But after that these things he must be released for a little while.*</u>**"**

I was delighted to see Satan cast into the bottomless pit, because I know there will be peace for that thousand-year period. What a time to be living if you are in Christ, because all of us who are saved will be reigning with Him for 1,000 years. Ezekiel saw the last battle before the Tribulation. Also, he gave details about it that John left out. Ezekiel is a prophet who had a very close encounter with the Lord. The hand of the Lord was upon him many times in his book. It is now time to go on my journey a little deeper in the word of God to see how God created the fourth creation. The earth was a total mess, because when Christ came down, there was a great earthquake where everything shook so bad that the mountains came down, and every wall fell. Then of course, God rained down fire from heaven. So everything was in a big mess for sure. Now God was going to create everything anew. I must take you to Isaiah, to see his view of the new fourth creation.

Chapter Twenty

ISAIAH'S VISION OF THE FOURTH CREATION

I saiah 65:17, 18, (vs. 17) *"For behold, **I create new heavens and a new earth**; And the former shall not be remembered or come to mind. (vs. 18) But be glad and rejoice forever in what I create; For behold,* **I create Jerusalem as a rejoicing**, *And her people a joy."*

God revealed unto me another piece of the puzzle to help us see the whole picture of His creation. Yes, another **secret** of the creation. *"For behold, I create new heavens and a new earth."* **This is not the same creation that will take place in Revelation 21**. To understand this, I must dig real deep into what Isaiah said in this passage. But first I need to know what happened before this came about. God is the master of all creations. What is God up to now? I need to go back in Isaiah's vision to see why there is a need for a new heaven and a new earth.

Isaiah 63:1,2, (vs. 1) "Who is this who comes from Edom, With dyed garments from Bozrah, This One who is glorious in His apparel, Traveling in the greatness of His strength?- <u>'I who speak in righteousness, mighty to save.'</u> (vs. 2) Why is Your apparel red, And Your garments like one who treads in the winepress?"

The Lord Jesus is describing Himself here, as He prepares for battle against Gog in Revelation 19:15. Isaiah 63:1 <u>"I who speak in righteousness, mighty to save."</u>) Is given insight into the future by the Lord God, to be able to witness this great battle.

*Isaiah 63:3, "I have trodden the winepress alone, And from the peoples no one was with Me. For I have trodden them in My anger, And one says, **'Do not destroy it,** For **a blessing is in it,**' <u>So will I do for My servants' sake, That **I may not destroy them all.**</u> (vs. 9) I will bring forth descendants from Jacob, And from Judah an heir of My mountains; **<u>My elect shall inherit it,</u>** And My servants shall dwell there. (vs. 10) Sharon shall be a fold of flocks, And the Valley of Achor a place for herds to lie down, <u>For My people who have sought Me</u>."*

God is going to spare some of His servants so that He can fulfill all of the prophecy of the Bible. Look real hard with me at these next verses, as we study what is to take place in the future. **Another piece of the puzzle is about to be revealed to us that will blow your mind shortly.** Please have an open mind as you read these things with me in our study. God said, (Isa.63:3) "*That I may not destroy them all.*" He left some of them alive to fulfill His prophecy. Then He said through Isaiah, (vs. 65:17) "*The former shall not be remembered or come to mind.*" We will not be able to remember anything from the old world when this happens. In this new earth that God creates in the future, there will be no devil or beast for a period of 1,000 years.

Nor will they remember that there ever was a devil but they will still need to obey the law of God because Satan will be released after the 1,000-year reign. Ezekiel's vision of the temple and all of its law will be in effect because Isaiah's and Ezekiel's visions are in the same duration of time. This is where their visions come together. The big difference in this duration of time is that Satan will not be able to deceive them into sinning, until he is released from his prison after the 1,000-year reign. But anyone who lives then will still have a free will.

Isaiah 65:19, "I will rejoice in Jerusalem, And joy in My people; The voice of weeping shall no longer be heard in her, Nor the voice of crying."

Now we can compare John's vision of the new heaven and new earth in these next few verses. In Isaiah's vision there is no weeping or crying. In John's vision this is also true. In Isaiah's vision, if there is no Satan, there would be no need for crying or weeping, because Satan can take nothing away from them. So far so good, in the comparison. Now look a little closer in the next verse in Isaiah 65: *(vs. 20) "No more shall an infant from there live but a few days, Nor an old man who has not fulfilled his days; For the* **Child shall die one hundred years old,** *But the sinner being one hundred years old shall be accursed."* In John's vision, there is going to be no more death at all. *Revelation 21:4, "And God will wipe away every tear from their eyes; there shall be no more death, nor sorrow, nor crying. There shall be no more pain, for the former things have passed away."*

In Isaiah's vision when *"the Child shall die one hundred years old,"* there is death mentioned in this verse. So this alone means that Isaiah's vision of the new earth is in a different duration of time than John's vision, because as you can see, in John's vision, *"there shall be no more death."*

In the next few verses in Isaiah, we can see that the everyday routine is carried out. They build houses, they plant vineyards, and they eat the fruit. They will have children born to them who will not cause them any trouble.

Isaiah 65:21-23, (vs. 21) "**They shall build houses** *and inhabit them;* **They shall plant vineyards** *and eat their fruit. (vs. 22) They shall not build and another inhabit; They shall not plant and another eat; For as the days of a tree, so shall the days of My people, And My elect shall long enjoy the work of their hands. (vs. 23) They shall not labor in vain, Nor bring forth children for trouble; For they shall be descendants of the blessed of the Lord, And their offspring with them."* Isaiah was probably happy when he was given this vision of the fourth creation of God. He could see that Israel was going to finally be placed in their own land to stay. Not only that, but they could again build their houses, plant their vineyards, and have children without anyone taking them from them. He saw that they would not labor in vain ever again.

The Lord showed me that Isaiah was not talking about the new heavens and earth in Revelation 21, but rather, the fourth creation, which is in the 1,000-year reign. By this time I am sure that the prophet Ezekiel was getting very excited, because he knew that God was going to let his vision begin to happen, the vision of the new temple. The Lord has now cleansed the earth of all corruption, therefore He now made a new heaven and a new earth, so that He could finish His prophecy. Ezekiel's temple was to be built, therefore the 1,000-year reign was to start. Satan and the beast were out of the way, so that means that the work of the new temple that Ezekiel saw could be completed without any interference from Satan.

The earth itself was not destroyed, just its surface, because the earth was to remain forever, for more than one reason. I could only imagine what it would look like this time. I am sure that it was very beautiful at that time, maybe just like God created it in the first creation. Everything looks good in this creation. Christ and His saints are there in their midst, to rule over those who were left. Israel was made a new nation that was not divided. Plus, they were able to build houses again, plant crops, and they were to have children. It was a time of peace like no one has ever experienced. No more Satan to bother them. Wow! What a time to live in. Let's look at Ezekiel's temple now.

Chapter Twenty-One

A NEW CITY, A NEW TEMPLE

E zekiel was not given any prophecy about the great white throne judgment. Instead, he was given a vision of the New Jerusalem and the heavenly temple that are to be set up on the earth. John saw in **Revelation 21:2, "Then I, John, saw the holy city, New Jerusalem, coming down out of heaven from God, prepared as a bride adorned for her husband."** What John saw here is not the same thing? We will discuss this later on. Abraham looked for this city also. **Hebrews 11:8-10, (vs. 8) "By faith Abraham obeyed when he was called to go out to the place which he would receive as an inheritance. (vs. 9) By faith he dwelt in the land of promise as in a foreign country, dwelling in tents with Isaac and Jacob, the heirs with him of the same promise; (vs. 10)**

for he waited for the city which has foundations, whose builder and maker is God."

We are to be looking for the city John saw. I can hardly wait until I can see it in person. Ezekiel spent the rest of his book describing this new City and new Temple. Before we look at this new City, and this new Temple, we must look for the part of history Ezekiel did not write about. In Revelation, John saw something Ezekiel did not see. John saw the great white throne judgment in which all of humanity was judged by their works that they had done while on earth.

Ezekiel 40:1-3, (vs. 1) "In the twenty-fifth year of our captivity, at the beginning of the year, on the tenth day of the month, in the fourteenth year after the city was captured, on the very same day the hand of the Lord was upon me; and He took me there. (vs. 2) In the visions of God He took me into the land of Israel and set me on a very high mountain; on it toward the south was something like the structure of a city. (vs. 3) He took me there, and behold, there was a man whose appearance was like the appearance of bronze. He had a line of flax and a measuring rod in his hand, and he stood in the gateway."

The Lord God was going to show Ezekiel what the new City and new Temple were going to look like in the future. Ezekiel spent the rest of his time writing about this experience. This was not the same City that John saw. If you are interested in reading about it, you can do that.

ISRAEL'S FINAL DESTINATION

Another **piece of our puzzle** is about to be unveiled in this book so that we can see with our eyes the beauty of God's handiwork. We only looked at a few of the Old Testament prophets in this book, so I am sure there is much more for us to explore that might be of help to us, but for now we are going to just study these two prophets, Ezekiel and John. Behold! I looked out of the window of my time capsule. I saw Ezekiel's vision coming to life over there. Through the eyes of the great prophet Ezekiel, we can see a new city with a very good constructed temple.

The first thing I saw was Gog and all the people with him were all buried, after the birds and beasts of the fields had their greatest feast, in which they were filled up till they could not eat any more. Then through John's vision, I could witness one of the greatest things of all. *Revelation 20:10, "The devil, who deceived them, was cast into the lake of fire and brimstone where the beast and the false prophet are. And they will be tormented day and night forever and ever."* Sad to say, Ezekiel was not given the part of the vision that John saw, where the beast and false prophet were cast into the lake of fire.

But the beauty of the whole thing is that we can see them both as God reveals them to us in these last days. Now through both of these great prophets, **another part of the puzzle** is revealed to us. Our God is so amazing. He is so patient, so loving and merciful. It is not my purpose to teach on the temple. I just brought up this subject for the purpose of showing the two different views of the new City, one came down from heaven, while the one Ezekiel saw was set up during the 1,000-year reign. The temple that Ezekiel saw was to come to the earth during the thousand-year reign with Christ. This would make sense, because there would be unsaved people who could not get saved because the Holy Spirit was lifted from the earth when the Rapture took place. In Ezekiel's vision, there were sacrifices that had to be made. There would be no need for that in the new heaven and new earth in Revelation 21, because John saw no temple;

Revelation 21:22, "<u>But I saw no temple in it</u>, for the Lord God Almighty and the Lamb are its temple."

It is my own theory that the new city Ezekiel saw was built by God's instructions in Jerusalem, during the 1,000-year reign with Christ. In Ezekiel's vision of the city, he saw the temple being built according to the design of the Old Testament law, whereas John saw no temple in his vision of the new city. Another reason is that during the 1,000-year reign, the saints will be judging the nations with Christ. There will still be sacrifices being made during that duration, but in John's vision there would not be anything like that done because Jesus' death on the cross took care of that forever! We could go on and on about that subject, but I just wanted to let my readers know were there two different cities they (John and Ezekiel) were talking about. To determine the differences between the two cities and two temples that the two prophets wrote about would require a lot of study time. Like I said, this is not my purpose to talk about that kind of detail in this book, but I may expound on it a little.

This New Jerusalem that Ezekiel wrote about is very interesting for us to look at because I believe this new city will be on earth during the 1,000-year reign.

Look at this verse in **Ezekiel 40: (vs. 2) "In the visions of God He took me into the land of Israel and set me on a very high mountain; on it toward**

the south was something like the structure of a city."

Ezekiel was taken by the hand of God in the spirit to see this city of the future. Notice one thing with me: he did not see this city coming down from heaven like John, but rather, Ezekiel was taken to the land of Israel in the distant future. Then God showed him exactly what the temple was to look like in the last days. Also he saw how it was to be constructed with all of the details of its beauty. This means that there is a period of time not mentioned in Revelation, for this Jerusalem that Ezekiel saw, to take place in the future. It has to take place probably after the last battle, at the end of the Tribulation, also during the 1,000-year reign with Christ. There is one reason that I can think of that might explain this dilemma. Ezekiel was given a vision of this great city and temple for God's holy people of the Old Testament, to be built some time in the future. The Lord God said that He was going to bring all of His people into their own land in Israel in the last days.

Watch with me as the puzzle comes together. John, who wrote Revelation, was the New Testament prophet, therefore God let John see the New Jerusalem descending out of heaven, which shall take the place of the old Jerusalem. If God showed Ezekiel that one, he would not have understood why his was to be built. In Ezekiel's vision in **43:5-7, (vs. 5) "The Spirit lifted me up and brought me into the inner court; and behold, the <u>glory of the Lord filled the temple</u>. (vs. 6) Then I heard Him <u>speaking to me from the temple</u>, while a man stood beside me. (vs. 7) And He said to me, '<u>Son of man, this is the place of My throne and the place of the soles of My feet, where I will dwell in the midst of the children of Israel forever. No more shall the house of Israel defile My holy name, they nor their kings, by har-lotry or with the carcasses of their kings on their high places.'"**

In Ezekiel's vision, **"the <u>glory of the Lord filled the temple</u>."** In John's vision, **Revelation 21:10, 11, (vs. 10) "And he carried me away in the Spirit to a great high mountain, and showed me the great city, the holy Jerusalem, descending out of heaven from God, (vs. 11) <u>having the glory of God</u>. Her light was like a most precious stone, like a jasper stone, clear as crystal."** The city John saw had the glory of God already in it, with many precious stones. His description was much different from Ezekiel's, because there are two different cities in these two books of the Bible. **Revelation 21:22, "But I saw no temple in it, for the Lord God Almighty and the**

Lamb are its temple." There was no temple in John's vision, but there was a temple in Ezekiel's vision. One city with a temple, one city with out a natural temple. In Ezekiel's vision of the temple, all of the Old Testament duties of the priests had to be performed, there had to be sacrifices made and the list goes on.

"BUT BE GLAD AND REJOICE FOREVER IN WHAT I CREATE"

*Isaiah 65:17, 18, (vs. 17) "For behold, **I create new heavens and a new earth**; And the former shall not be remembered or come to mind. (vs. 18) But be glad and rejoice forever in what I create; For behold, I create Jerusalem as a rejoicing, And her people a joy."*

God is always in the creation mode. He is always creating new things. In this Chapter He is going to create new heavens and a new earth. This new heavens and new earth are not the same ones John saw in his vision! You might think that I am out of my mind. That is okay, but let me show you what I am talking about. This new heavens and new earth are going to happen during the thousand-year reign. This, my friend, is going to **be the fourth time that the earth will be created anew**. When we went back in time, we saw the other three creations. Now we shall see yet the fourth creation as we read this chapter. *"For behold, I create Jerusalem as a rejoicing, And her people a joy."* (vs. 18). In this Chapter Isaiah saw God creating a new heavens and a new earth, and Jerusalem also being created anew. By the way, this is the same New Jerusalem and temple Ezekiel saw. Think about what had already taken place so far. The earth was a total mess from the destruction of the major battle that took place between God and Gog. Fire came down from heaven and destroyed Gog and company. It took Israel seven months just to bury the dead bodies. The earth was almost in total destruction. But God was not done. He needed to fulfill some prophecy from the Old Testament, therefore He said that He was going to create everything anew. To do this, He was going to start from scratch, by making new heavens and a new earth. He said that **"the former shall not be remembered or come to mind."**

Chapter Twenty-Two

EZEKIEL'S VISION FULFILLED

The greatest battle ever fought in history is now behind us. Satan, the beast, and the false prophets are in the lake of fire to be tormented day and night. The judgment of God has taken place, so now what? In my spirit I was just thinking, "What would Ezekiel be saying to God? Would he be saying, 'What now, Lord God? My vision that you gave to me many years ago, when is it going to be fulfilled?'" I am sure that God would answer him in a gentle way, "Watch what I will do!"

We humans think that we have everything figured out, but sadly, we know very little about how God's prophecy works. I know very little myself about them, so I have to rely on the Holy Spirit to give me insight into their mystery. I am sure that Ezekiel was looking down from heaven when he saw God's judgment taking place, wondering when his prophecy was going to take place. Did John leave out a chapter, or was that chapter already written in the Old Testament, waiting to be fulfilled? God did not throw away the Old Testament prophecies. They will come to pass, for the word of the Lord is steadfast and sure. As I looked into the two accounts about the end of time, the Holy Spirit showed me that Ezekiel's temple was to be built in that future place, just after the last battle at the end of the Tribulation. For Ezekiel's prophecy to take place, it needed people to perform its task. God left instructions in Ezekiel's vision for how He wanted it to be built. So we must look into Ezekiel chapters 40-48.

A NEW TEMPLE

Ezekiel 40:2,3, (vs. 2) "In the visions of God He took me into the land of Israel and set me on a very high mountain; on it toward the south was something like the structure of a city. (vs. 3) He took me there, and behold, there was a man whose appearance was like the appearance of bronze. He had a line of flax and a measuring rod in his hand, and he stood in the gateway."

Now Ezekiel's vision is being fulfilled in the future right after the battle at the end of the Tribulation. I know that Ezekiel would be beaming with great joy while he witnessed his vision taking place right before his eyes. The Old Testament prophecy of Ezekiel is finally coming to pass. God promised the Jews, the Israelites, that they would possess the land forever. He also would be in their midst always. Now is the time for that to happen! There is no more devil or beast or false prophets left in John's vision of this temple that was to be built. Everyone who was left alive had peace and joy, for the tempter was no longer around! Now they could build the perfect temple of God, according to His instruction given through Ezekiel's vision.

Ezekiel 40:4, (vs. 4) "And the man said to me, 'Son of man, look with your eyes and hear with your ears, and fix your mind on everything I show you; for you were brought here so that I might show them to you. Declare to the house of Israel everything you see.'"

Ezekiel was given great detail of how the temple was to be built. Now in the book of Revelation, this temple is to be built with all of the details given to Ezekiel in that vision. John has no clue of what is going on at this time, because he did not have a vision of that temple. He did not see a temple in his vision in Revelation 21. The reason he did not see it is because that was for the Old Testament prophecy to be fulfilled before Chapter 21.

The wall would be the first thing that was constructed, according to Ezekiel's vision. This temple is built somewhere in Israel, but not on the spot where the New Jerusalem will come down from heaven. There could be no better time to build a city than this time in Revelation, because there would be no opposition from the enemy, which is burning in the lake of fire. But why build another temple now? Does it make sense to do that before the great white throne judgment? Is God going to give the Jews another opportunity to give their lives to Him completely? I just had to look at Ezekiel one more time, so I could show you the whole piece of the puzzle.

Ezekiel 39:25-29, (vs. 25) "Therefore thus says the Lord God: **'Now I will bring back the captives of Jacob, and have mercy on the whole house of Israel;** *and I will be jealous for My holy name- (vs. 26) after they have borne their shame, and all their unfaithfulness in which they were unfaithful to Me, when they dwelt safely in their own land and no one made them afraid. (vs.* 27) When I have brought them back from the peoples *and gathered them out of their enemies' lands, and I am hallowed in them in the sight of many nations, (vs. 28)* then they shall *know that I am the Lord their God, who sent them into captivity among the nations, but also brought them back to their land, and* **left none of them captive any longer.** *(vs. 29) And I will not hide My face from them anymore, for* **I shall have poured out My Spirit on the house of Israel,' says the Lord God."**

We read these scriptures earlier in this book, but I thought it would help us understand what we are talking about now. At this time in the future, God is going to pour out His Spirit on all of Israel. This sounds like Israel is going to have another chance to be what God called them to be: His chosen people. As the hand of the Lord was upon Ezekiel, He showed Ezekiel every detail of how He wanted the temple to look like. Look over there, can you see in the spirit the wall being built around the temple? Why, the width of it is about 10.5 feet. I could see everything being laid out according to the vision Ezekiel saw. Every part of the temple was built exactly like it was in his vision. This temple that Ezekiel saw in his vision was being built for all of those who were under the law in the Old Testament or maybe for those of the New Testament who still lived by the law, or both of them. I say that because of what I can see in the temple and the things that take place.

First, there is a place were sacrifices are prepared. *Ezekiel 40:38, 39, (vs. 38) There was a chamber and its entrance by the gatepost of the gateway, where they washed the burnt offering. (vs. 39) In the vestibule of the gateway were two tables on this side and two tables on that side, on which to slay the burnt offering, the sin offering, and the trespass offering."* If you do not believe that this is going to happen or if you think that this is the same vision of John, think again. In John's vision he saw no temple. Why? Because in his vision of the New Jerusalem, there would be no need for any sacrifices. In Ezekiel's vision, there is a need for the sacrifices. Look with me in the spirit. Behold the beauty that Ezekiel saw of the temple in a vision. Behold, it is coming to pass right before our eyes! Every detail that Ezekiel saw was being performed to a perfection from his vision.

> *Ezekiel 43:5-7, (vs. 5) "The Spirit lifted me up and brought me into the inner court; and behold, the glory of the Lord filled the temple. (vs. 6) Then I heard Him speaking to me from the temple, while a man stood beside me. (vs. 7) And He said to me, '***Son of man, this is the***

**place of My throne and the place of the soles
of my feet, where I will dwell in the midst of
the children of Israel forever."**

*Ezekiel 43:11, "And if they are ashamed of all
that they have done, <u>make known to them the
design of the temple</u> and its arrangement, its
exits and its entrances, its entire design and all
its ordinances, all its forms and all its laws.* **Write
it down in their sight, so that they may keep
its whole design and all its ordinances,** *and
perform them."*

In (vs. 7), <u>*"Son of man, this is the place of My
throne."*</u> God told Ezekiel that this was the place of
His throne, where He will dwell with them forever.
Everything will be done exactly how God wants it to
be. At this time there will be no devil because he is
burning in the lake of fire! I believe that God is going to
pour out His Spirit on all of Israel just before the final
judgment of God. *Ezekiel 39:29, "And I will not hide
My face from them anymore; for I shall have poured
out My Spirit on the house of Israel, says the Lord
God."* So that He can fulfill His promise to them, and
that is why the temple is being built for them, so that
they can perform all their duties to the Lord God, by

serving Him in this temple and city. One thing for sure, they will be serving God until The Great White Throne Judgment, just before Revelation chapter 21 takes place. As I was studying Ezekiel 39:21, I was trying to figure out when the temple was to be built. I had to read it again and again until I finally got a revelation of its meaning. Please read it with me now: *Ezekiel 39:21, "I will set My glory among the nations, all the nations shall see My judgment which I have executed, and My hand which I have laid on them."* According to this scripture, it will take place after the last battle of the great Tribulation, also during the 1,000-year reign with Christ. God's glory will be set among the nations in this new temple that Ezekiel saw in a vision. There will be people from all nations who are left, because God is not done with His total plan. He promised that He would bring all of Israel back to their own land for good.

This is why He needed the temple to be built, because most of His people were still under the law, therefore, there was still a need for sacrifices to be made by them to God for their sins. John was not given this part of the vision because this part of the vision belongs to the prophets of the Old Testament. John was not allowed to steal their thunder. Now that we understand those things, we need to move on to the things done in the temple. But first, we are not told how long this temple will be here on the earth. God told them that they would remain loyal to Him from that day forward.

It will last for thousand of years, then it will last beyond that until the white throne judgment. Now back to the temple in Ezekiel's vision. We left off talking about (vs. 7), *"Son of man, this is the place of My throne,"* and that is why I explained the above verses to you, so that we could establish where we were in this vision. As I said, both of the visions go hand-in-hand, so you can see with me that we have to go back and forth to get the whole picture of what God is showing to us. This temple that we can see here in Ezekiel's vision is different than John's vision of a New Jerusalem, which had no temple, as I stated before.

In Ezekiel's vision there are to be sacrifices made. *Ezekiel 43:18, "And He said to me, 'Son of man, thus says the Lord God: "These are the ordinances for the altar on the day when it is made, for sacrificing burnt offerings on it, and for sprinkling blood on it."""* Although Satan is no longer there upon the earth, everyone who is left on the earth still has his or her old nature. The only difference is that they will not be able to blame the devil for whatever action they choose to do. God said in *Ezekiel 39:29, "And I will not hide My face from* them anymore; for I shall have <u>poured out My Spirit</u> <u>on the house of Israel, says the Lord God</u>."

It is not clear when this will take place, but it will take place. There will be those who are saved and those who are not, so God instructed who may enter the temple in *Ezekiel 44:9, "Thus says the Lord God: '<u>No foreigner, uncircumcised in heart or uncircumcised</u> <u>in flesh, shall enter My sanctuary, including any for-</u> <u>eigner who is among the children of Israel.</u>'"* In this temple there are laws governing priests: 44:10, 11, *(vs. 10) "And the Levites who went far from Me, when Israel went astray, who strayed away from Me after the idols, they shall bear their iniquity. (vs. 11) Yet they shall be ministers in My sanctuary, as gatekeepers of the house and ministers of the house, they shall slay the burnt offering and the sacrifice for the people, and they shall stand before them to minister to them."*

Living in the city and the temple will be different for the Israeli people in this future time zone because their enemies have been destroyed. Also the devil will not be there to tempt them either, until after the 1,000-year reign with Christ. There are many things that will happen in this temple of the future. If you want to learn more, you can read the rest of the scriptures in Ezekiel 39-48. I just needed to show you that this prophesy of Ezekiel's vision must come to pass in that duration.

Look at the water flowing from under the threshold in *Ezekiel 47:1, 2, (vs. 1) "Then he brought me back to the door of the temple; and there was water, flowing from under the threshold of the temple toward the east, for the front of the temple faced east; the water was flowing from under the right side of the temple, south of the alter. (vs. 2) He brought me out by way of the north gate, and led me around on the outside to the outer gateway that faces east; and there was water, running out on the right side."* God also took him out of the east side with a line in his hand. He took Ezekiel out into the water, 1,000 cubits each time. First it reached his ankles, then it reached to his knees, then it came up to his waist. After that, Ezekiel could not reach the bottom of the river because it was over his head. The Lord took him back to the bank. This special river brought healing wherever it went, even along its banks: *47:12, "will grow all kinds of trees used for food; their leaves will not wither, and their fruit will not fail. They will bear fruit every month, because their water flows from the sanctuary. Their fruit will be for food, and* **their leaves for medicine.**"

But in John's vision of the New Jerusalem, there will be no sickness, or pain, or death. So that is another reason these verses above are for the temple in Ezekiel's vision only. In Chapter 48, the division of the land is discussed, then the gates of the city are named. Then finally: *Ezekiel 48:35, "All the way around shall be eighteen thousand cubits; and the name of the city from that day shall be: THE LORD IS THERE."* {Just a note, Zion could be the place for Ezekiel's city to be built} *Isaiah 66:7, 8, (vs. 7) "Before she was in labor, she gave birth; Before her pain came, She delivered a male child. (vs. 8) Who has heard such a thing? Who has seen such a thing? Shall* **the earth be made to give birth in one day? Or shall a nation be borne at once?** For as soon as **Zion** **was in labor, She gave birth to her children."**

This Fourth Creation of God took me a long time to get all of the information together, because there are many scriptures to look at on this subject. With the Holy Spirit's help, I was able to get it done. Now my question to God was answered: there is a Fourth Creation of God hidden in the scriptures. I cannot tell you how long it will last, but it will remain there on earth at least until the great white throne judgment. Before I take you to the fifth creation of God, I would like to remind you what just took place in this Fourth Creation of God.

I personally have not ever heard about this Fourth Creation of God, therefore I know that it will be hard for anyone else to believe that it will exist in the future, but if you have read what I wrote about it so far, you too will know that it will happen. Not just because I said it, but because it is in the scriptures. God's word will come to pass whether you or I believe in it or not. Remember what I have written about this Fourth Creation: It is to take place after the great Tribulation, because God said that He had some of His chosen ones whom He saved for a purpose, to bring them back to their own land. Both Ezekiel and Isaiah saw by the Spirit where Israel would become one nation during that time. Also Ezekiel's vision of the temple would be built in that creation.

In the Fourth Creation, God created a new heavens and a new earth, in which Christ reigned with His saints for 1,000 years. It was here that Ezekiel's temple was to be built for Christ to reign from. At the end of it, Satan will be released for a short time and will deceive many people to come against it. I will talk more about these things in the next chapter.

THE SAINTS REIGN WITH CHRIST 1,000 YEARS

Revelation 20:4, "And I saw thrones, and they sat on them, and judgment was committed to them. Then I saw the souls <u>of those who had been beheaded for their witness to Jesus</u> and *for the word of God, who had not worshiped the beast or his image, and had not received his mark on their foreheads or on their hands. And <u>they lived and reigned with Christ for a thousand years.</u>"*

What will it be like to reign with Christ for 1,000 years? Just the thought of reigning with our Lord for 1,000 years gives me goose bumps! A thousand years without the devil around would thrill my soul to pieces! It would be a time of peace like I have never witnessed in my entire life. The scripture above did not say how many thrones he saw, but he did say, *"And they lived and reigned with Christ for a thousand years."* So there could be a huge amount of thrones. I believe there will be no sickness or any other health problems during that duration, because Satan is locked up in the bottomless pit. I know that Ezekiel's vision of the temple will be built according to God's instruction after the Tribulation; maybe during the time of the seven years while Israel is burying the dead bodies from that great battle.

The scriptures did not say for sure, but it was going to be there for the 1,000-year reign for sure, because there is nowhere else in the scriptures for this to happen. There will be many people living at that time other than Christ and His saints, because this needs to happen so that Christ and His saints rule for that entire time. There are not many scriptures talking about the thousand-year reign. First, let me ask you a question, "This thousand-year reign, is it a literal thousand years of our time? Or a thousand years according to God's timetable?" A thousand years is a day in God's timetable, so if this thousand years are in God's timetable, it would be 362,000 in our timetable. Whether it is just an ordinary thousand years or 362,000 years, it does not matter, it is just an idea that I wanted to mention. We are not going to know all of the answers to these questions until we get to heaven.

I know that the saints of God will reign with Christ for these 1,000 years. The other people who made it through the Tribulation, who did not worship the beast or his image, will be living outside of the camp of God. They will continue having babies and living a normal life. But they are blessed, because Satan is locked up in the bottomless pit for 1,000 years. Since Satan is locked up in the bottomless pit, there may be no sickness or other health problems either, or possibly there may not be any death during that time. I am just giving you my thoughts, because the Bible does not say too much on the matter. All I know for sure is that the saints will be ruling over them for 1,000 years.

There will be no temptations for them because Satan is locked up, therefore there may be no one sinning in that duration of time. There will be no more wars or jealousy until the thousand years are finished. Those who came through the Tribulation period will surely feel different without the influence of Satan deceiving them.

If I could witness this thousand-year period, I would observe something different about those people. I would see them getting along really well. There would be no fighting among themselves or stealing from one another. In the camp of God, I did notice that there was no night there, no darkness at all. The brightness of God's presence was light enough to light the whole camp. With all of the people working together, nothing was impossible for them. I am sure that there would be no murders or killing of humanity in that time period, either. There would be no jails or prisons, possibly. The population of the people grew at alarming rates, as we will see in the next few verses. Another thing I noticed was that everyone who was born during that 1,000-year period had no knowledge of sin. But I am sure that the saints of God who were ruling with Him warned them that the tempter, Satan, would be released soon.

SATANIC REBELLION CRUSHED

Revelation 20:7-10, (vs. 7) "Now when the thousand years have expired, <u>Satan</u> will be released from his prison (vs. 8) and <u>will go out to deceive the nations</u> which are in the four corners of the earth, Gog and Magog, to gather them together to battle, whose number is as the sand of the sea. (vs. 9) They went up on the breadth of the earth and surrounded the <u>camp of the saints and the beloved city.</u> And fire came down from God out of heaven and devoured them. (vs. 10) The devil, who deceived them, was cast into the lake of fire and brimstone where the beast and the false prophet are. And they will be tormented day and night forever and ever." When the 1,000-year reign of Christ ended, Satan was loosed from his imprisonment. His main purpose was to "*deceive the nations.*" If all of the people were saints, then how would Satan be able to deceive them? That is an interesting statement. There are only four verses, but those four verses give us very little detail as to what happened. As soon as Satan is released from prison, he does not waste any time, he goes to all parts of the earth to: "*deceive the nations.*"

There is not really a period of time given here for how long it took him to deceive the nations, so it could have taken him a long time to do that. It was a large number of people, though, so many, no one could count all of them. This battle right here is the second great battle in the book of Revelation. This battle is the last battle recorded in the book of Revelation. The first battle is just before the 1,000-year reign, as I already pointed out. The second battle is shortly after the 1,000-year reign of Christ is over. After a long time studying these two battles, I received a revelation from the Lord, the key secrets to understanding the differences between the two of them.

It was after those things that the writer of Revelation said, *(Revelation 20:11,12) (vs. 11) "Then I saw a great white throne and Him who sat on it, from whose face the earth and the heaven fled away. And there was found no place for them. (vs. 12) And I saw the dead, small and great, standing before God, and books were opened. And another book was opened, which is the Book of Life. And the dead were judged according to their works, by the things which were written in the books. (vs. 13) The sea gave up the dead who were in it, and Death and Hades delivered up the dead who were in them. And they were judged, each one according to his works."*

Revelation 20:14, 15 (vs. 14) "Then Death and Hades were cast into the lake of fire. This is the second _death._ _(vs. 15) And_ _anyone not found written in the_ _Book of Life was cast into the lake of fire."_

Again, I am not sure how much time elapsed between verses 10 and 11 of that chapter. It could have been a long time, or a short time, but God said that Israel will abide forever. This will take us to the fifth creation of God.

Chapter Twenty-Three

THE FIFTH CREATION OF GOD

Revelation 21:1, 2, (vs. 1) "Now I saw a new heaven and a new earth, for the first heaven and the first earth had passed away. Also there was no more sea. (vs. 2) Then I, John, saw the holy city, New Jerusalem, coming down out of heaven from God, prepared as a bride adorned for her husband." Finally God is going to create a new heaven and a new earth for the fifth time. God is going to create it perfect so that He can make this earth and heaven ready to be His new home. Heaven on earth, if you will. The New Jerusalem is seen coming down from heaven. What a place this will be! We have already studied and learned that this New Jerusalem is not the same one Ezekiel saw. The transition from Revelation 19:6 to 21:1 is not clear how long it will take or what happened just before we

entered the final new heaven and new earth. Just like the gap between the first two verses in Genesis chapter 1, there is a gap in time from the end of the Tribulation to the beginning of Revelation 21. There will be a large number of years between those two chapters.

During the last creation, I talked about many things that would take place before we enter this last creation of God. So far I could not find when that creation would end or just maybe the children of God in that creation were able to enter the next one, by the grace of God, because He said that they would carry on for ever and ever.

Revelation 21:5, "Then He who sat on the throne said, 'Behold, I make all things new.' And He said to me, 'Write, for these words are true and faithful.'" God is going to make the ultimate new heaven and new earth for His New Jerusalem, so that it would be perfect for His new kingdom. Then in *(vs.6), "And He said to me, 'It is done! I am the Alpha and the Omega, the Beginning and the End.'"* I believe that this will be the final creation for this earth. When God said, *"It is done!"* He meant it. He is going to make the earth perfect, better than ever. *Revelation 21:9, "Then one of the seven angels who had the seven bowls filled with the seven last plagues came to me and talked*

with me, saying, 'Come, I will show you the bride, the
Lamb's wife.'"

Come with me to see the bride of the Lamb. Look at
her, she is the most beautiful bride I ever laid my eyes
on. We can see her by the description that John saw,
from the high mountain. *John 21:10, 11, (vs. 10) "And*
he carried me away in the Spirit to a great high moun-
tain, and showed me the great city, the holy Jerusalem,
descending out of heaven from God, (vs. 11) having
the glory of God. Her light was like a most precious
stone, like a jasper stone, clear as crystal."

I wish that I could witness this spectacular sight
right now, the way John saw it. I am sure that it would
have surprised me greatly. Just look in the spirit right
now; you cannot miss it! A great, large city coming
down from God, directly out of heaven. This alone
would cause me to fall on my face before the Lord in
awe. From its brightness, my eyes are almost blinded.
He goes on to tell about the dimensions of all its walls
and gates. You can read them later if you want. I want
to skip to verse: *18, "The construction of its wall was*
jasper; and the city was pure gold, like clear glass."
Then look at verse: *21, "The twelve gates were twelve*
pearls: each individual gate was one pearl. And the
street of the city was pure gold, like transparent glass."

Does this cause you to want to go there? It does that for me for sure! Ezekiel did not say anything about the streets being paved with gold in his vision. As I said earlier in this book, Ezekiel saw a different city than John. Also there was no temple in John's vision. Look at the glory John saw in the next few verses, *(vs. 22) "But I saw no temple in it, for the Lord God Almighty and the Lamb are its temple.* (vs. 23) *The city had no need of the sun or of the moon to shine in it, for the glory of God illuminated it. The Lamb is its light."* When this takes place there will be no sun or moon because: *"The Lamb is its light."*

If you remember we saw that one other time, on our journey back to the very beginning of time. There was no sun or moon mentioned there either, because God's light kept everything growing until Lucifer rebelled against God, along with other angels who followed him. I mention this again to help you remember what we studied so far. *(Vs. 24) "And the nations of those who are saved shall walk in its light, and the kings of the earth bring their glory and honor into it. (Vs. 25) Its gates shall not be shut at all by day (there shall be no night there)."* In Ezekiel's vision, the gates were not always opened, like the ones here in John's vision. It was God's intentions for the earth to be inhabited in the beginning of time. It might be hard for you to understand what I am about to reveal to you, so please bear with me a little while longer.

There will be other nations here in Chapter 21 because for us to reign forever with Christ, there needs to be some other people here on the earth, for us to reign over. For surely, we are not going to reign over one another. We will be higher than the angels of God though, but God wants men and women to be there for the earth to replenish itself. *John 21:26, (vs. 26) "And they shall bring the glory and the honor of the nations into it. (vs. 27) But there shall by no means enter it anything that defiles, or causes an abomination or lie, but only those who are written in the Lamb's Book of Life."* Who are they in the verse above? *(vs. 24) "And the kings of the earth bring their glory and honor into it."* They only bring the ones who are saved. (Vs. 27) says, *"There shall by no means enter it anything that defiles, or causes an abomination or lie."* John sees a pure river of water of life in the next chapter, which is different from what Ezekiel saw. Read John's vision, then we will compare it to Ezekiel's vision of the river.

Revelation 22:1, 2, (vs. 1) "And he showed me a pure river of water of life, clear as crystal, proceeding from the throne of God and of the Lamb. (vs. 2) In the middle of its street, and on either side of the river, was the tree of life, which bore twelve fruits, each tree *yielding its fruit every month. The <u>leaves of the tree were for the healing of the nations</u>."*

Ezekiel 47:1, "Then he brought me back to the <u>door of the temple;</u> and there was water, flowing from under the <u>threshold of the temple toward</u> the east, for the front of <u>the temple</u> faced east; the water was <u>flowing from under the right side of the temple</u>, south of the altar." In John's vision there is no temple (John 21:22), but as you can see there is a temple mentioned four times alone above in (Ezekiel 47:1). This again is why there has to be two different time periods to these accounts, because God's word does not contradict itself! In (Ezekiel 47:8, *"Then he said to me: 'This water flows toward the eastern region, goes down into the valley, and enters the sea. When it reaches the sea, its waters are healed."* In Ezekiel's vision, the water enters the sea; in John's vision, (*Revelation 21:1*) *"Also there was no more sea."* There is one more thing that I want to say. It is in (*Revelation 22:3*), *"<u>And there shall be no more curse,</u> but the <u>throne of God and of the Lamb shall be in it</u>, and His servants shall serve Him."* These people will be saved but will not be transformed like us because they are saved after the rapture of the church. They will be in human body form like Adam and Eve, with the exception of one thing: their bodies will be able to live forever, because they made it through everything, therefore these ones are able to eat the fruit of the tree of life; thus they could live forever.

The tree of life was there in the Garden of Eden, but because Adam and Eve took of the tree that was forbidden, the tree of life was taken out their reach. In that creation, God gave Adam and Eve a choice to make. He said that they could eat of any tree except one. If they would have chosen that option, they would not have received the sentence of death. The "tree of life" will be available in this fifth creation. *John 22:2, "In the middle of its street, and on either side of the river, was the tree of life, which bore twelve fruits, each tree yielding its fruit every month. The leaves of the tree were for the healing of the nations."* I am not adding to or taking away from this great book of Revelation, I am just giving my opinion of what I was able to interpret from it, as I was studying its content, by allowing the Holy Spirit to teach me the secrets of God's creations.

In the New Jerusalem, nothing shall enter it that (vs. 27) *"causes an abomination or lie."* That could mean there is a chance that the ones who are not living in that New City could defile themselves somehow, only because they will still have a free will. *(Vs. 22:27) "But there shall by no means enter it anything that defiles, or causes an abomination or lie, but only those who are written in the Lamb's Book of Life."* I personally think that life will go on in this fifth creation, people will be born, and they will build houses. But God will be on the earth with us forever. I hope that you have a better understanding of the five creations of God, now that you have read this book. If you do not agree with it, that is okay. Everyone has a right to their own beliefs, but make sure you believe in the word of God no matter what.

Chapter Twenty-Four

THE TRANSFORMATION OF
THE BODY

What happens to our earthly body? That is a good question. I hope that I will be able to shed some light on that subject for you. Of course, we are made up of spirit, soul, and body, as we have studied so far in this book. It was God's intension to make man in His image in the beginning of His creation. God did that when He created the spirit man in the first chapter of Genesis. This spirit man that God created will last forever for sure. Now when God formed a man, who was made of the dust of the earth, that man (Adam) was formed to last forever, but with one exception: he had to obey one command that His creator gave to him. He was not to eat of the tree of the knowledge of good and evil. If he ate of it, he would lose his ability to live forever. He broke that commandment in Genesis 3:6.

Now that his body had the sentence of death, it needed to be redeemed so that it could someday be restored to an incorruptible body once again. So you might ask, how is it possible for this to happen? I am glad that you asked. I would be happy to tell you how that is possible, my friend. God is so amazing. He thought of everything even before we were born into this world. He knew that the earthly man was going to mess up by eating of the forbidden fruit, so He had a plan to fix the problem by the woman's seed that was in Adam's wife. I talked about this in an earlier part of this book. God told the serpent that His Seed was in the woman, therefore it would be in enmity against his seed, through the seed that was in the woman. God knew that He had to send His only Son into this world to save humanity from hell. God knew that Eve's seed was going to be carried all the way to Mary, Jesus' mother, in the New Testament. It is in Mary's womb that the Holy Spirit placed the seed of Jesus at the appointed time.

God's only Son came to the earth to show us the way to get to heaven. He showed us by His example how we should live and what we needed to do to enter heaven. He became our sacrifice on the cross to take away our sins forever. Without receiving Him as the Lord of our life, we could not enter heaven when we die. The next plan for God was to show us how to die the right way. Therefore, we could have a proper burial, then have a righteous resurrection with Christ Jesus our Lord. Now by Jesus' example, we can have a body like His. He made it possible for us by His resurrection, so that our physical body will also change into a substance that will be like His when our bodies will be resurrected some day from the grave.

Jesus came to the earth to get an earthly body like ours, but with a twist. He lived a perfect life on this earth, in an earthly body, to show us how we could do the same thing if we would be buried in the baptism of His death, burial, and resurrection. Because when Jesus rose from the dead, He came up out of that tomb a new person. The earthly body was now changed into a material that would last forever that would be indestructible. Even Mary Magdalene was told by Jesus not to touch Him, because He did not go to His heavenly Father yet, to be glorified. The same thing will happen to us some day, but first when we die, our earthly body will return to the earth it came from.

Someday God is going to raise our earthly body up from the grave and it will be made of the same material as our Lord's body! Just briefly, let me explain this the best way I can by using some scriptures in context. First I must bring to your attention one thing before I start. In the scriptures that I want to use, Jesus was comparing the first earthly man, Adam, to the second Adam (Jesus), in the way they were to be changed to an incorruptible person.

First, I would like for you to read **1 Corinthians 15:35-41**, so that you will be able to have better knowledge on this subject: People are always curious about this subject. A lot of people do not have a clue of what he is talking about, because they can only discern in their natural way of thinking.

They are saying, **(vs. 35) "But someone will say, 'How are the dead raised? And with what body do they come?'"** Well, Paul told them the answer first with things they could relate to, such as farming: **(vs. 36) "Foolish one, what you sow is not made alive unless it dies. (vs. 37) And what you sow, you do not sow that body that shall be, but mere grain -- perhaps wheat or some other grain. (vs. 38) But God gives it a body as He pleases, and to each seed its own body."**

The seed that you hold in your hand to sow cannot come to life unless it dies when it is planted. All you can do is plant it. You cannot give it a body of your choice. God is the one who gives it a body as it pleases Him. In the next three verses, Paul explains how there are different kinds of flesh, also he says that there are different celestial and terrestrial bodies. God is not limited by the amount of different bodies there are, because it is up to Him what kind of body He wants it to be. **(vs. 39) "All flesh is not the same flesh, but there is one kind of flesh of men, another flesh of animals, another of fish, and another of birds."** Paul says that there are four kinds of flesh mentioned here. They are all different because God chooses them to be that way. Not only has that, but look in the next two versed. There you will see yet more kinds of flesh. **(vs. 40) "There are also celestial bodies and terrestrial bodies; but the glory of the celestial is one, and the glory of the terrestrial is another. (vs. 41) There is one glory of the sun, another glory of the moon, and another glory of the stars; for one star differs from another star in glory."**

This means that there are (vs. 40) "**celestial bodies,**" which pertains to spiritual bodies in the heavenly realm. They are made of a different substance than the (vs. 40) "**terrestrial bodies,**" which pertains to the earthly bodies (natural bodies) here on the earth. Paul talks in farmer's terms first, showing his readers the principle of death and life, planting and harvest. He explains to us that if we plant a seed in the ground, it cannot produce anything unless it dies first. He says that the one who sows the seed is not the one who gives it the body of what it shall become. It is God who determines what kind of body it shall have.

Paul then tells his readers that there are different kinds of flesh that each body could have, as well as the different glories that they have. Each one is different in its own way. Now Paul is leading up to tell his readers how the dead bodies are raised from the dead in the next verses. By now he hopes that they can understand what he is talking about.

1 Corinthians 15:42-43, (vs. 42) "So also is the resurrection of the dead. The body is sown in corruption, it is raised in incorruption."

The body dies, it is sown in the ground to decay, it is corrupted, but when God raises it up, He makes it whole again, it is made alive, and therefore it is raised in incorruption. Paul is trying to get his readers to see the comparison between the seeds they plant and the way humans are sown in the ground. Look at what he is saying: just like the seed you planted in the ground, it was sown in dishonor, it had to die, it was weak, but when it died, it came back up through the ground in power, therefore, it was able to get strong. The same thing happens to the natural body: **(vs. 43) "It is sown in dishonor, it is raised in glory. It is sown in weakness, it is raised in power. (vs. 44) It is sown a natural body, it is raised a spiritual body. There is a**

natural body, and there is a spiritual body." That little seed that you planted was useless until it was planted in the ground, but look now, it came back up out of the ground a little stem only to become strong, therefore it was able to reproduce itself. **(vs. 45) "And so it is written, 'The first man Adam became a living being.' The last Adam became a life-giving spirit."** Paul says that there are two Adams here: the first Adam was made out of the earth, who became a living being. But the last Adam, who is Jesus Christ, became a life-giving spirit (Romans 5:12-17). Through the first Adam, everyone who is born on this earth was born a natural physical person and took on his nature, therefore was born in sin. But Paul says that Jesus Christ, who is the last Adam, became the one who gives us spiritual life. **(vs. 46) "However, the spiritual is not the first, but the natural, and afterward the spiritual."**

This verse is taken out of context many times by different people. If you read the next verse, Paul explains what he is saying here. Paul is saying that the first man, Adam, was made of the dust of the earth. Everyone who is made of the dust of the earth is made like him, having borne the image of the first Adam. But the second Adam, Jesus Christ, who was the spiritual in (vs. 46), came after the earthly man Adam. Now Jesus is the last Adam, because after He was crucified, dead, and buried, He arose from the dead, and became the life-giving spirit who can give life to all. Jesus was the first to be raised from the dead in a resurrected, transformed earthly new body. The first Adam was made a fleshly body that had the sentence of death, without hope of a resurrection until the second Adam (Jesus) came to take on a fleshly body. Then when Jesus was crucified and planted in the ground, something happened to that earthly body that He had. On the third day it took on a new form when it was resurrected from the dead. God gave it a new material that was indestructible, incorruptible and became glorified when Jesus went back to His Father. The same thing is going to happen to the believer's earthly body when it is planted in the grave. At a specific time it will be raised from the dead in an incorruptible body also!

(vs. 47) "The first man was of the earth, made of dust; the second Man is the Lord from heaven. (vs. 48) As was the man of dust, so also are those who are made of dust; and as is the heavenly Man, so are those who are heavenly. (vs. 49) And as we have borne the image of the man of dust, we shall also bear the image of the heavenly Man."

Everyone who is made of the dust, like Adam, is like him in every way. So also is everyone who is born again will bore the heavenly, they are like "**the second Man is the Lord from heaven.**" Everyone who is not born of the Spirit will not "**bear the image of the heavenly Man.**"

1 Corinthians 15:50-57, (vs. 50) "Now this I say, brethren, that flesh and blood cannot inherit the kingdom of God; nor does corruption inherit incorruption. (vs. 51) Behold, I tell you a mystery: We shall all be changed - (vs. 52) in a moment, in the twinkling of an eye, at the last trumpet. For the trumpet will sound, and the dead will be raised incorruptible, and we shall be changed. (vs. 53) For this corruptible must put on incorruption, and this mortal must put on immortality. (vs. 54) So when this corruptible has put on incorruption, and this mortal has put on immortality, then shall be brought to pass the saying that it is written: 'Death is swallowed up in victory.' (vs. 55) 'O Death, where is your sting? O Hades, where is your victory?' (vs. 56) The sting of death is sin, and the strength of sin is the law. (vs. 57) But thanks be to God, who gives us the victory through our Lord Jesus Christ. We shall all be changed."

Yes, there is coming a day that our mortal bodies will be drastically changed, where our earthly body will be made of incorruptible material that will last forever.

Death will not come to it anymore. We will have a body at that time like the body Jesus had after His resurrection from the dead. Jesus is the first one ever to have the privilege of that transformation, of being born from the dead. (His fleshly body was made incorruptible before anyone else, so that no man can brag that he was the first one to do that.)

1 Corinthians 15:57, "But thanks be to God, who gives us the victory through our Lord Jesus Christ."

This completes our tour of the five creations of God. It was a long journey to take, but every moment of it was fantastic for me. I hope it was for you, too. Even though we did not go on a real trip, it was a real experience because you were interested along with me in finding out how things were created, outside of popular belief. By examining the scriptures in a closer way, with an open mind, you could find answers that you might not have thought of otherwise. This was a very difficult book for me to write because I was taught that the earth was only a few thousand years old. But the fact remains, the earth is probably million of years old. I knew that there had to be some misunderstanding in the interpretations by Christians on the age of the Bible.

For that reason, God laid it on my heart to write this book so that I could understand why there is so much controversy on this subject, and to help me to get this information out to the public and other Christian believers. I know there will be many who will say that I am out of my mind, and that is okay. They thought the same things about Jesus also. They said He was a madman, but we know that Jesus is our savior and the King of Kings, regardless of what the world thinks. I do not care what the world thinks about me either.

May God Bless You,
Big Al Casto

ABOUT THE AUTHOR

My name is Alan Casto, I consider myself as co-Author of this book because it was given to me by inspiration of the Holy Spirit of God. I have been working on this book for several years now and was told to have it published by God.

I was born in East Liverpool Oh. I graduated from high school from Stanton Local in Irondale, Oh. I then went into the US Naval Reserves in 1967. After serving two years active duty I got a job with General Motors I worked there almost 37 years, I then retired. I got married in 1971 to my wife Ann, we had three wonderful children and 8 grandchildren and one great grandchild. We have now been married almost 44 years.

I came to know the Lord Jesus as my personal Savior in 1971. We have been through many storms throughout those years of marriage but the Lord saw us through all of them. I had a near death experience one day when I tried to end my life, I actually died and went through a tunnel of light where an angel of God spoke to me and said, "God is not done with you yet, I am going to send you back to the earth." Then I immediately my spirit was back into my earthly body. I jumped out of my bed and told my wife what had happened to me; and my life has never been the same sense that time. I rededicated my life to the Lord. Sense that time the Lord has given me visions that has come true, He has given me new understanding of His word and told me to write them down. This is my third book that I have written, and it is the only one that I was told to have published for now. I am going to publish the other ones when I am told to do so.

Big Al Casto

CPSIA information can be obtained at www.ICGtesting.com
Printed in the USA
LVOW12s1945051214

417409LV00004B/4/P